MAKE A $IX FIGURE INCOME DOING Hair

How To Do It, Really.

ALAN DANIELS

This book is dedicated to my mentor,
Johnny Hernandez, for unselfishly
Teaching me everything I know about
This industry.

Chapters

Is This the Industry for Me?

It would be presumptuous to list the traits one must have to be successful in this industry. Diversity is what makes the hair industry interesting for those who work in it and for those who patronize it. Success is also a relative term.

It can be said, though, that those who do reach some level of success have certain characteristics in common with other successful industry professionals.

The following list of characteristics is submitted to provoke thought and to give the reader a general list of traits that seem to be associated with success in this industry. It is in no way intended to be a list of prerequisites for success.

> **Am I a people person?** It's no mystery that this industry is based on maintaining constant contact with people and providing services to them. When it comes to this trait, I think I can fairly certainly

say that if you don't enjoy being with people, it may be very difficult to make it in this business.

Am I shy? I have trained all types of people in this business. Some have been very outgoing, and some have been very shy and soft-spoken. I will say that those who are a bit more gregarious tend to have an easier time in this business, but it is not a "must" for success. If you are generally on the shy side but have a genuine interest in this industry, you can still do well as a hair stylist—if you remember a few key things. You need to "act" as if you are outgoing, and you need to project a confident image.

You do not have to change your personality or alter who you are to be a successful hair stylist. You do need to change your behavior, though. A behavior change is all it is. I'll explain. Clients buy what they see. That goes for the products we sell, and that goes for us, too. People buy our image—or the image they have of us. If your clients feel that you are confident in yourself, they will have more of a tendency to put their trust in you. If you come across as insecure, you will make them nervous and your job will be a lot harder. Speak up (project your voice), watch your posture, dress the part, and be decisive in your comments. Again, you do not need to change who you are, just how you act.

Do I enjoy creative outlets? As a hair stylist, you will have numerous opportunities to express your creative nature. You'll be placed in unusual situations, and coming up with new ideas and problem solving will be daily activities. If you embrace this sort of thing, you will do well. If you don't, think about whether it is something you can learn to enjoy.

Am I open to learning? Because this is a technical trade, the industry is structured in such a way that the experienced people teach the new people. The experienced people pass down information to the new people and teach them something each day. Every stylist can name someone who was instrumental in his or her development. A willingness to learn is vital. Remember that just because someone teaches you something doesn't mean that you have to "own" that idea and make it a part of who you are. You just have to be willing to learn it in the first place and to give everything a chance.

Am I willing to work every Saturday? Every salon is different, but the industry standard is a workweek that runs Tuesday through Saturday. There are many clients who can only come in for an appointment on the weekends, and I don't mean Sundays. You will most likely have to give up the wild Friday night outings if you want to be fresh for the biggest day of the week.

Can I stand on my feet all day? Don't worry. This seems to be a concern for more people than one would think. If I took you to your local gym and told you to jump into a step aerobics class, you would find it difficult at first. At the end of a couple months, you would be used to the class, and the physical requirements wouldn't be much of a concern. The physical demands of the hair industry are much the same. You will get used to it very quickly. Here's some advice: When you start in the hair industry, you'll want to make two key purchases—a quality set of shears and a really good pair of shoes. You may also consider a padded mat to stand on while you work.

Can I commit to three years? This industry moves at a different pace for everyone. Many things affect it—environment, education, personal ability, attitude, and more. One thing is for sure, though: nobody "arrives" at success straight out of hair school. Many, many people are enjoying successful careers in the hair industry. It can work for you, too. But you have to give it time to happen. Give yourself, and the industry, three good years, and don't expect instant gratification.

Do I need natural artistic ability? No. As with anything else, if you enjoy it, you will get good at it. I guarantee it. I had absolutely no natural ability for doing hair. I learned everything from step one. Improving my skill set wasn't work; it was fun. If you seem to have that natural ability to start with, it's a bonus! Just make sure you enjoy it, and you'll do well.

Do I enjoy it? This is a hard question to answer if you have never spent any time in a salon environment. Many people like the idea of doing hair but don't really know if they could actually do it for a living. Well, go and find out! If you are thinking of a career in the hair industry, do a little homework before you jump in.

Find a salon in your area and ask if you can "hang out" for a few hours on the next few Saturdays. Ask if you can help out in some way, even if it's just offering drinks and magazines to clients. There is no pay for this types of research, so don't ask for it. It will give you a good feel of what the day-to-day job might be like and whether or not it might be right for you.

If at all possible, you need to do this before you enroll in hair school. It's always great to enjoy what you do for a living, but in this industry, enjoying what you do is vital. If you don't enjoy this business, you won't be as likely to spend the extra time and money to attend a weekend trade show or to buy educational material. If you don't enjoy this business, it will be difficult to "get into it," and getting into it is what it takes to make it in the industry—and employers and clients can always tell whether or not you're into it.

Internship

To achieve success in the hair industry, you need to set yourself apart from your peers. There are literally hundreds of thousands of licensed hair stylists in this country, and they're all trying to make it big. Every one of them wants to stand out from the crowd and increase his or her odds of success. The best way to do that is to start your career the right way by obtaining some sort of internship or mentorship from someone who's already established in the industry.

> **What is an internship?** There are different kinds of internships, and they are all beneficial. Some people know established professionals in the industry and ask if they can train under them. Other people contact salons to ask if they offer some sort of training program for future employees. Internships can range from "one-on-one" training with a mentor to a large-scale structured program that was established to break in and train new

stylists. It doesn't matters which kind of internship you get into—just get into one!

What's the role of Hair/beauty School?
It's a common misconception that hair school will teach you what you need to know so you can go out and find a job. You must first know the role of Hair/beauty School. Every school has a responsibility to the state to maintain a certain passing ratio for its students. If a certain amount of a school's students do not pass the state examination, the school will be affected negatively. So what do you think the main focus of the beauty school is? It's to get you through the curriculum so you can pass the test. The school has no vested interest in your becoming a talented and successful hair stylist. That does not mean that the instructors don't care—they do. But you must realize that their job does is not to make you successful.

Each school has a staff of qualified instructors who have the ability to make you talented and successful, but when they're teaching a regular curriculum, they don't typically have the time to do so. They can't share all of their personal experiences in the industry with you.

Their job is to teach you the basics and to prepare you for the state examination. If you finish school and don't have the ability to obtain a job and function in the industry, don't blame the school. Take a good look in the mirror. Take responsibility.

When should I get an internship? Now! The sooner the better. Most beauty school students don't know that an internship may be available to them while they are in hair school or even before they start. You need to know that obtaining an internship is vital to increasing your odds of success in the hair industry. It is very difficult for most people to jump into an industry and figure out what works without any help at all. Why would you try it in this industry? Before you start working, it is vital that you put yourself in a position to receive a real-life education of what the hair industry is all about. If you have already finished school, you may have to backtrack a bit. It will be worth it in the end. Look at the large picture. Don't wait another day—get into a program now.

How do I get an internship? Every salon owner is looking for the right people to add to their staff. If you are in hair school or just about to start, no salon owner will expect you to know much. Do not make the mistake of thinking that you need to get better before you approach a salon or an individual about an internship. All salon owners are looking for the same sort of people. We look for people who want to be successful in the hair industry and are willing to work for it. We are looking for the people who are hungry.

Go to several different salons to get a feel for different environments. Maybe have a service done and see how the people work together. Do some homework before you approach a salon. Once you find one or two salons that interest you, ask to speak to the manager or owner about a possible internship. Let them know that you are willing to sweep hair or set up for stylists if they let you watch and attend any classes or advanced education programs. Let them know you are willing to work for free. All you want is the opportunity to learn and to get a realistic picture of what the hair industry is all about. Working for free may be hard for some. Consider this: Education costs everyone something. In this case, all it will cost you is a bit of your time. You can give your time to salon owners who share their experiences with you. It's a good trade. You may only be able to go to the salon a few hours each week. It doesn't matter. If you walk into a salon and offer yourself up like this, very few owners will tell you "no."

When you try to get more education before you get out of school, you set yourself apart from many other people in the industry, and you demonstrate that you want to make it. You show that you are willing to give up your time in order to increase your odds of success. You are hungry! Salon owners will snatch you up if you show them what you're about. Many of these internships will turn into paying jobs, too. The salon owners will be willing to train you because you may become a motivated and well-trained employee who will rise through the ranks in their salon. They have a vested interest in making you talented and successful.

Don't let people scare you. People will tell you that you are not allowed to work in a salon or to be in contact with clients until you have a license. It is true that each state has its own set of rules when it comes to working in a salon and having contact with clients. Find out what the laws in your state are. But don't be discouraged. There are many things you can do to help in a salon environment without violating state rules or risking your future license. The important thing isn't what you do at the salon. The important thing is that you are there getting real-life experience. Every day you spend there is one day that you are ahead of the crowd.

Where Should I Work?

When you are done with your schooling, you need to work. But how do you know what kind of salon you should work in or whether or not a salon is right for you? Everything we do in this business either increases or decreases our odds of success. The initial choice you make as to where you will work can help you greatly, or it can slow you down on your road to success.

> **Demographics.** When looking for a salon to work in, you need to consider who your clientele will be. Go to the salon and look at the guests. What is their average age? Are there more women than men? How many people live in a one-, three-, and five-mile radius of the salon? Find out from the salon owner what the average income per household is in the area. This will tell you if the clientele will support your prices or the prices of the salon. For example, if a new upscale salon is opening in an area where the

average haircut is twenty dollars and the salon you want to start at is charging fifty dollars per haircut, it may take you a long time to build your clientele, regardless of how optimistic the salon owner may be. Similarly, if you want to specialize in color services but the salon you want to work in caters mostly to men, it may not be the salon for you. The vast majority of color services are still sold to women. Find out as much as you can about your demographics.

Distance. Is the salon you want to work in a reasonable distance away from your home? Will you get to work on time every time? A reliable employee is more valuable to an employer than a talented employee is. If you are an amazing "rock 'n' roll" hairdresser full of talent and charm, but an employer doesn't know if he or she can count on you to be there for your clientele, then you are a liability, not an asset, and your days will be numbered. Make sure the salon is not too far away from where you live, or make sure you have the means to move closer to the salon.

The "feel" of the salon. What does the person at the desk look like? What do the other staff members look like? Is there an obvious dress code of some kind? Can you tell the staff from the guests? Does the staff look professional? The first impression you get from the front desk and the other staff members is the same one your clients will get when they walk into the salon. Make sure your first impression of the salon is professional and warm. A good salon environment is essential to building a strong clientele. You may be wonderful at what you do, but if the clients don't like the salon, they will eventually leave.

Your growth potential. What does the salon do to build a new stylist? What can you expect the first month, the sixth month, and the second year? Ask for details. Does the salon have a way to track your growth and evaluate where your education should be focused? What sort of marketing does the salon participate in? What can you do to promote yourself within the salon? Take some responsibility for your success, and get involved.

What are the other staff members like? How long have they been there? If the salon has any kind of level system for pricing, how long does it take for the average employee to advance? Find out how many people have left the salon in the last year. If people are constantly leaving, there may be a problem.

Materials. What does the salon provide to its employees? Ask about business cards, station product usage, shampoo-area supplies, tools, capes, and other supplies. You need to know these things to know what you must obtain when you start.

Benefits. Does the salon provide any sort of benefits (medical, dental, retirement, paid vacation, retail bonuses, etc.) to their employees? Do you need to be at the salon for a certain period of time to take advantage of these benefits?

Deductions. Does the salon deduct service/backbar fees from your check? These fees are usually deducted to help the salon cover costs for things like towels and laundry, shampoo-area supplies, station products, some marketing costs, and interns or assistants These fees are very normal and are necessary for most salons. Find out how they are calculated and how they are deducted from your check.

Contracts. Does the salon require an employee to sign some sort of contract or agreement? It is very normal for a salon to require a prospective employee to sign something. Every salon needs some level of protection. Many people will use a salon to build a clientele and then take that clientele somewhere else. No business can grow if this happens over and over. All salons need to protect against this sort of thing. That is why agreements are necessary in most salons. Have any agreement reviewed professionally by an attorney before you sign it. I will discuss contracts in greater detail later in the book.

The Critical Consultation

This chapter is likely the single most important chapter in this book. This is not a subject that you need to just read about; it's a subject you need to "own." I have done my best to format this information in a way that will make sense to the reader. Toward the end of the chapter, I will put it all together in one large example to show its application. Please read this chapter many times and know that I called it the "Critical Consultation" for a good reason.

Every hair stylist knows that the consultation is a part of any hair service. It happens when the guest arrives, and it's used to find out what the guest would like us to do on that particular visit. Once the consultation is done, we start the hair service, and off we go.

I can honestly say that in my twenty-five years in the hair business, I've spent more time training staff on this subject than on any other. The initial consultation is your first and best opportunity to connect with your guest and to "set the stage" for the appointment in general.

Here's an example of a typical consultation that you might see in any salon. In our example, Sandy will be the hair stylist and Jane will be the guest. Sandy has just finished with her last guest. She returns to her station and cleans up so she can start on Jane, who is waiting in the reception area. Sandy is ready for Jane. As Sandy picks up her cutting cape, she shouts out and waves to Jane.

"Jane, come on back, "she says. Jane obeys, walks over to Sandy's chair, and sits down. Sandy moves to the back of the styling chair, puts the cutting cape on Jane, and says, "So, what are we doing today?" They talk a bit and decide on a haircut, and then Sandy says, "Let's go get you shampooed." The consultation is done, and the service starts. The only way this could've been worse is if it had been the guest's first visit to Sandy. We'll talk more about the difference between a first-time client and a retuning client as we progress.

If a stylist just goes through the motions of a consultation and focuses on starting the service, he or she will miss out on a huge opportunity and do a terrible disservice to the guest.

The stylist who takes the consultation process for granted and doesn't use it to "set the stage" will find it very, very difficult to be successful in the hair business. I hope I've been clear. A correct consultation is critical.

I'm going to list the key points to cover in a consultation. Key points are, quite simply, the things that you must do during the consultation process. You should do these things deliberately because they are all connected and vital to a correct consultation. Let's talk about a new guest who's coming in to see you for the first time.

> **Give a professional greeting to your guest.** Never invite your guest to "come back" to your workstation! Always go out to the waiting area and walk him or her back personally. Nothing says "lazy" or "apathetic" more than a stylist who calls out for her guests. This practice is, quite honestly, very unprofessional, and it could even be seen as "low-class." Please don't be that stylist. Remember that you're trying to project an image of yourself at all times. Ask yourself if your actions are getting that picture across to your clients. If the answer is "no," make a change.

When you seat your guests in the styling chair, **do not put a cape or drape on them yet.** We drape our clients when we perform a service, not when we consult. This point is important because when the drape goes on the guest, it seems like the service has begun, and the guest will stop listening. You use this time to set the stage not only for the appointment, but also for yourself.

Walk out from behind the chair and get in front of your guest. Lean up against the mirror wall or against your station furniture; it doesn't matter what you lean on—just get in front of your guest. You will conduct your consultation from this point of view. For some reason, this seems to be one of the most uncomfortable things for a stylist to do. Get over it! It's that important.

Never conduct a consultation by talking into the mirror from behind the chair. The goals of conducting a consultation are to establish how you do business, to give the guests new ideas, and to make the guests feel as if they are in a professional's hands. You need the guest to really hear you when you talk. When you're face to face with your guests, they're more likely to listen. You also want your clients to get the feeling that you are not like the rest of the hair stylists they've seen in the past. You take the first step toward making that distinction when you get out in front of a client during the consultation. This action requires confidence, but more importantly, it shows confidence. Now you can talk to the client about the service he or she will receive.

There is a format that public speakers use when they're trying to get a point across. It is broken up into three parts. Firstly, you should tell your audience what you're going to tell them. Secondly, you should tell them. Lastly, tell them what you told them. We will use this format during the course of our appointment.

After you have talked about what will happen and agreed upon a course of action, the real fun begins. **Let your guest know what will happen during the course of the appointment from A to Z.** (This is the "tell-them-what-you're-going-to-tell-them" step.) You will do this with confidence, not with arrogance. You will do this just like a dentist would describe an upcoming procedure—not in a cold and detached way. This is the point when you truly establish who you are, what you do, and exactly how you conduct your business. If this is done properly, the client will walk away with the impression that her appointment was handled professionally and that she was in capable hands from the beginning to the end. She will feel comfortable returning again and referring others to you. Most importantly, she will be more likely to accept your recommendations.

Tell your guest that you like all of your clients to know what to expect when they sit down with you. Say that you realize you're just providing a haircut, but that throughout the course of the appointment **you will throw out new ideas that might work for your client as they come to you.** Remember: One of your goals with any consultation or simple haircut appointment is to offer three new ideas every time. It's not important that the clients take your recommendations right away; it's important that you plant the seeds of the ideas in their heads. Besides, which hairdresser will build a larger business? The one who always has new ideas every time he or she schedules with you, or the one who says, "So, what are we doing today?"

Let your guests know that you will also **tell them about products that will keep/get their hair healthy.** Usually, those products will be a good shampoo and conditioner unless the client's hair requires a treatment of some sort.

Let your clients know that when the appointment is finished, you will show them the styling products you used so they can duplicate the style at home. Do not talk about each product you use as you are styling unless the client asks you to. Most stylists feel too much like salespeople when they do this, and it's not comfortable for the guest either. Rather than talk about the styling products, use the styling time to essentially give the client a styling lesson. Really show the client what you're doing and tell her why you're doing it as you style. Take the time to teach your clients something that they can use at home. If you do this, it will seem natural for you to tell your client about the styling products you used.

Let your guest know that when she's happy with her hair, the two of you will **determine how soon she needs to return and schedule that appointment before she leaves.** (See the chapter on pre-booking for details.) Explain briefly that your schedule is very tight and that all of your clients prebook when possible. Your guest should get the feeling that you do that for her benefit, not for your own.

Finally, you should ask, **"Is that OK with you?"** Let her say "yes." All of these **key points** happen in the "tell-them-what-you're-going-to-tell-them" section of the appointment. This is not a drawn-out lecture or conversation; you're not explaining your position or why you do what you do. She already knows why you do these things—you told her. You want her to know what she can expect throughout the appointment with you and how you conduct your business. Now you can put the drape on her and proceed with the service. You will cover the "tell-them" portion of the appointment as you perform her ser-vice and as you talk about everything you're doing. We will talk about the "tell-them-what-you-told-them" portion of the appointment at the end of this chapter.

I have offered a lot of information in a short period of time. At this point, it might seem difficult to sort it all out in a useful way and to actually implement these techniques when working with your clientele. I understand. So to make this whole process easier, let's put it all together in one example consultation so you can get a better sense of what this would really be like when you do it yourself. This example deals with a new first-time client.

You are ready to see your next guest. She is waiting in the reception area. You walk up and **give her a professional greeting**. You then walk her back to your workstation. You do not put a drape on her. **You walk out from behind the chair and position yourself in front of her so you can begin your consultation.** You will talk about the particular service she is interested in and decide on the details of her service. Once you have made a decision about the service, it's time to "set the stage" and tell her what she can expect. It might go something like this:

"I know this is your first time seeing me, so I'd like to sort of lay out how this whole visit will go and let you know how I tend to work. I don't want there to be any surprises. I always start with a hair analysis and recommend treatments if you need them. I know we're just doing a haircut today, but as ideas come to me I'll throw them out to you, just to give you something to think about for later. When we're done with your haircut and we start to style your hair, I'll give you a very detailed explanation about how I'm doing the styling. I really want you to be able to duplicate what I do here at home. When we're all done, I'll show you the products I used to make the style happen. The last thing we'll do is set up your next appointment. My schedule is pretty tight, and that's the best way to make sure my clients get in when they need to. Is that OK?"

"Great, let's get started."

That's all there is to it. This should take no more than sixty seconds to explain. Be yourself, and have fun giving your new guest her service. In sixty seconds you will have successfully instilled confidence in your new client, let her know she is dealing with a professional hair stylist, and opened the door so you can accomplish all of the items on your checklist of things that you need to do to build your business and to keep her happy. I cannot emphasize enough how important it is that you hit every key point on your checklist and leave nothing out. It is equally important that you do this with every new client—no exceptions. Hairstylists have a tendency to decide ahead of time which key points their client will likely be open to and only cover those points with her during the consultation. That is a *huge* mistake. Be consistent, stay professional, and do everything you need to do so your business can grow. Remember: you're in this for the big picture—not just for the picture of today.

List of key points to cover:

Professional greeting

Do not drape yet

Walk around and get in front of your guest

Decide on the service—do the consultation

Set the stage—let her know what to expect

Hair health suggestion

New ideas for her hair—for example, color services.

Styling lesson

Styling products

Prebook her appointment

Ask, "is that OK?"

Doing this kind of consultation is sometimes easier with a first-time client. Our existing clients are sometimes a different story. Our existing clients already know us. In fact, they'll know if we didn't do the consultation this way during their last appointment or, for that matter, during the last two years. You might be thinking, "What if she asks why I'm standing in front of her all of a sudden? I can't run down that whole list with her before I start her service. She'll think I'm crazy. I'm going to look like a fool!" I've heard some of those comments while teaching this subject. But relax— it's actually easier to complete a critical consultation with an existing client. You are still going to hit all of the key points you need to cover, but you will handle it a bit differently because you'll already have a relationship with the guest. If your guest makes any comments about the new way you are conducting your appointment or asks you why you are doing things differently, keep your answers short and direct. Use humor, and keep the mood light. Don't make excuses; it makes you look unsure of yourself. Above all, have confidence. This example deals with a repeat client.

You walk up to the reception area to bring Lucy back to your workstation. You give her a professional greeting and bring her back to the styling chair. You don't put the drape on her. You intentionally walk around in front of her to talk about what you're going to do instead of talking to her through the mirror.

She asks, "Why are you standing there—is something wrong?"

You laugh and say, "No, I'm tired of talking to people in the mirror. That's all." You then decide what you will do that day. Instead of setting the stage as you would with a new client, you let your existing client know you'll be doing things a bit differently from now on. Make sure to do that in a way that doesn't sound rehearsed or contrived. Use your personality to do it, but don't miss any of the key points. Do not prejudge your client just because you already know her. Hit every point—no exceptions. Setting the stage with your existing client might sound like this:

"So, Lucy, today I'm going to do a hair analysis on you when we're in the shampoo area. We're having a special on treatments, and if you could use one, I'll let you know. Also, when we style today I'm really going try to explain exactly what I'm doing. I've been hearing that a lot of my clients are having a hard time making their hair look the way I do it in the salon, so today you get a styling lesson."

This is as far as I would go to set the stage with an existing client. You will still cover the products used during the styling and go through your prebooking process, but you will do it without giving your client advanced notice. Don't be surprised when Lucy asks you what all of the new stuff is about. In fact, be ready for it. Have a simple answer ready. For example, you could say, "I've been doing some new training and reading lately, and I feel like I could really be taking better care of all my clients, so that's what I'm going to do." Whatever you say, keep it simple and don't make any excuses. Have confidence.

I would like to cover something regarding setting the stage and how it applies to all of your guests. You will set the stage with every guest who sits down in your chair, but you will only need to do it one time. You will do it on the first appointment with any first-time guest you see, and you will do it only once with all of your existing clients that you service. Throughout the course of your appointment you will hit every key point, but you're only going to talk about them one time. If you stood up in front of each guest at the beginning of every appointment and told her what you were going to do, you would look a little foolish. After you have let a guest know how the appointment will proceed and how you conduct business, you just do it every time and with every guest. The only time you will go through the formalities of setting the stage will be when a new guest sees you for the first time. All of your guests will simply become accustomed to how you work, and trust me when I tell you that they will adapt to it and respect you for it.

When listing all of the key points that you will hit throughout the course of the appointment, I mentioned two that I feel require more of an explanation. They are letting the guest know what products were used on her during the styling process and prebooking her next appointment. These are two very important subjects to cover in any initial consultation, but they take place at the end of the appointment, and specific training is required for each subject.

> **Styling products**. (This step happens in the tell-them-what-you-told-them portion of the appointment.) When you are completely done providing a service for your guest, you will walk her to the reception area. You will walk every guest up to the front when you are finished with his or her service, because a professional good-bye is just as important as a professional greeting. Then, you will turn away from your guest, not say a word, walk over to the retail product displays, and pick up each product you used on your guest during her styling. Also pick up any

shampoo, conditioner, or treatments that you recommended to her. Place those products on top of the reception desk. Quickly tell your guest which product is for what purpose, how much to use, and other necessary information. Don't make a product education seminar out of it— just let her know what you used and why you used it. Do not pause at all. Simply say that she should let the receptionist know what she wants to do with the products, and then drop the subject. You will immediately move on to prebooking her next appointment. I have dedicated a whole chapter to the subject of retail sales, so I will not go into too many details on the subject. Remember this, though: When it comes to retail products, we do not sell—we just tell. You are not going to ask her if she would like to take any of the products on the desk home with her, and you're not going to wait around to find out if she does. You are simply going to explain why you recommended them, drop the subject, and move on to your next key point.

Prebooking. I have also dedicated an entire chapter of this book to the subject of prebooking. You can reference that chapter for all of the details on the subject. I will talk a little about this key point now and show how it flows into the end of each appointment.

So you are at the end of the appointment and have just dealt with the styling products. You will now walk straight over to the scheduling computer or your appointment book and say, "How many weeks do you usually go in between appointments? What's normal for you?" (See prebooking script and procedures in the prebooking chapter.) You will find that most people will be quite relieved to see that you are not interested in finding out whether or not they are going to take products home. It should be obvious to her that you are more interested in scheduling her next appointment than in selling her something. You will then schedule her appointment and say a warm good-bye.

You should now have a pretty clear idea of how appointments will flow. You should be clear on all of the key points that you need to hit during every appointment. However, I would like to leave you with a few ideas that may not be obvious to you.

Hitting all of the key points listed in this chapter and incorporating them into the normal routine of every appointment will not come naturally to anyone. Every stylist I have trained has struggled with one point or another. Everything in this chapter must be practiced and learned. You can't simply read the material and expect things to change. The first thing you need to do is see the logic of each key point and understand that everything is connected when it comes to providing services and building a business. The next thing you must do is practice. Think about what we have covered here. Many of these concepts may be new to you, and some of them are actually scripted. Do not practice these new ideas on your clientele. If you do, you might receive a negative comment or experience an embarrassing situation, and that could cause you to abandon your new skills. Use your clientele to become very skilled at these key points—but practice first. Practice with a friend, a family member, or another stylist. Fumble your words with those people—not with your guests. After you practice these new skills, you will be able to demonstrate confidence with your guests. Confidence, not arrogance, is the key you need to make all of these skills work for you and to build your business.

Commission or Rental

Commission or rental—that is the question. It is the most basic business decision you must make as a hairdresser. Which choice is right for you? In the beginning, you will most likely find it necessary to obtain a commission position in a salon so you can build a solid clientele. Your ultimate goal, however, is to establish a rental position so you can maximize your earning potential and make as much income as possible.

Commission: Hairdressers working on a commission basis receive a percentage of the business they generate in the salon, and the salon retains the rest. You should be very clear about the commission rate before you accept a position. As part of the commission transaction, the salon should provide the basic necessities for a stylist. The basic necessities should include clientele, a station and backbar products, business cards, and chemicals for services. The salon should also cover any immediate business expenses. The hair stylist is expected to provide his or her own profes-sional tools. A commission position is ideal for someone starting out in the industry.

Rental hairdressers normally pay a set weekly rent for the use of a salon chair, the shampoo area, and common areas. Your rental pay-ment should also include access to a recep-tionist for screening and handling appoint-ments. The rental hairdresser is responsible for all of the other business expenses, including all chemicals needed to provide services, busi-ness cards, a station and backbar products, and any other business expenses. Essentially, a rental hair stylist simply leases a space within the salon and is responsible for everything else, but he or she will keep 100 percent of all the money he or she generates. The salon will only receive a weekly rent payment from the stylist. A rental position is ideal for the stylist who has an established clientele.

When is the right time to go rental? Quite simply, the right time is when you can afford to stop working on commission and would make more money by doing rental work. You need to be renting your own salon chair if you expect to significantly increase your earning power. As with everything in this business, you will not make this decision based on your feel-ings or based on your best guess. You must conduct a business analysis to determine if the time is right for you to go rental. To conduct a business analysis, use the following steps and mark down your calculations on a ledger or a spreadsheet. (The following ledger is provided.)

Commission or Rental

Comparison sheet

Column #1

(Weekly rental income)

_____

Column #2

(Weekly commission income)

_____

Column #3

(Rental expenses)

_____

_____Total

_____Total

(a.) _____

(b.) _____

(c.) _____

(d.) _____ **Total**

- -

(Subtract)

Column #1 total _____

Column #3 total _____

_____ Net weekly rental income

_____ Average weekly commission

income (column #2)

X_____ Commission?   X_____ Rental?

Let's say you are working on a commission basis and you want to know if it's time to consider renting/leasing your own workstation and becoming fully independent. We will go through this process step by step to come to a conclusion.

Firstly, determine your potential earning power as a renter by estimating your average gross weekly rental income. To figure out this total, look at your appointment schedule, count back eight weeks, and add up the total amount of income you earned for both you and the salon during this period of time. (Don't look at commission split—add up the total amount of service business you brought into the salon before your split.) Divide this combined income total by eight to arrive at a weekly average for that eight-week period. We will call this your average gross weekly rental income. In other words, this would be the total amount of money you would have received as a renter under the same circumstances. Write down that income figure under column one on your ledger. (I'm only using eight weeks as an example. If you want to have an even more accurate average weekly income figure, repeat the same process using a longer period of time instead of eight weeks. Try using a twenty-five-week period of time. That will give you an average over a six-month period. Arriving at an accurate weekly average income is the most important step in this process.) Don't forget to consider what time of year you are using to calculate your average. For example, don't average your weekly income over the Christmas season and believe that it will represent the average you would receive throughout the rest of the year.

Next, calculate your average weekly commission income. To figure out your average weekly commission income, add up all of your commission paychecks before taxes for the last eight weeks. This figure will usually appear on your check stub as "gross income" and will be a higher amount than the actual amount of your checks. (For future reference, the amount that you actually receive on your check is called your "net" or "take-home" income.) Now divide your total gross income amount by eight to arrive at a weekly average for that two-month period. We will call this number your average weekly commission income. Write down that number under column two on your ledger. Next calculate your average weekly expenses. These would be the expenses that you would have incurred if you had been working on a rental basis. When you work as a commission stylist, though, the salon pays these expenses for you.

Look back at the same eight-week time period and write down exactly how many chemical services you performed and what types of services they were. Find out exactly what the cost of each of those services would have been if you had paid for the product yourself. Don't just calculate the cost of color; you also need to calculate the cost of developers and activators to arrive at an accurate cost amount. If you use processing caps or other supplies to perform these services, be sure to include the costs of those items in your calculations, too. Add up the total eight-week cost of these chemicals and supplies. Divide that total number by eight to arrive at an average weekly cost of chemical supplies. Write down your chemical expenses total under column "three a." on your ledger.

Then you should calculate what your weekly chair rental rate would be. If the salon you are working with offers chair rental, just ask what the weekly rate is. If they don't offer rentals, you will need to check with other salons in the area to find out what their weekly rental rates are. The amount may vary a bit, so try to come up with an average price per week and use that number. (If it is necessary to move to another salon to obtain a rental position, be sure to stay as close as you can to where you are currently working. Try to rent at your current salon if at all possible.) Write down your weekly chair rental rate under column "three b." on your ledger.

Estimate your total cost for station products, backbar products, business cards, and any other miscellaneous expenses that you can think of. Remember that you will typically be responsible for all of these expenses in a rental position. These kinds of expenses are easier to calculate on a yearly basis because you don't buy them every week. So estimate your total annual cost for all of these expenses and divide that number by fifty-two to arrive at an average weekly cost for these consumables. Enter this average weekly cost under column "three c." on your ledger.

Calculate your total average weekly expenses. Add up all of your weekly expenses under column rows "a.," "b," and "c" in column three on your ledger to arrive at your average total weekly expenses. Enter your total average weekly expenses under column three on the line labeled "total."

Subtract your total average weekly expenses (column three on your ledger) from your average gross weekly rental income (column one on your ledger) to arrive at your average weekly rental net income. This would be the total amount of money you would have left over at the end of the week if you were working on a rental basis. Compare your average weekly rental net income with you average weekly commission income (column two on your ledger). If your average weekly rental net income is larger than your average weekly commission income, it may be time to consider a rental position instead of the commission position you now have; if not, you need to build your clientele base awhile longer.

You need to weigh all of these considerations and make your decision based on logic. Do not allow emotion or fear to dictate your decisions or to decide your fate for you. You should make this decision, like all others in this industry, based on what is best for your business.

There is one final point to consider if you decide to go rental: It may be necessary to you to leave your current salon. As I said before, try to rent a chair at your current salon if at all possible. But a move may be necessary if your current salon does not offer chair-rental positions or simply will not offer that opportunity to you.

If you leave your current salon, you'll probably wonder whether or not your clientele
will follow you. Yes, they will! If you have been
doing hair long enough to build a large and
loyal clientele and you provide superior services, you should be confident in the abilities
and skills you have acquired. For the most
part, your clients come into that salon for you.
Don't be fooled into thinking that the salon is
the main draw for your clients; the relationship you have built with them is a much stron-
ger draw.

You do need to be aware that when you
relocate, you will always lose a small percentage of your clientele, even if you move right
next door. I have found that, on average, a
hairdresser will lose about 10 percent of his
or her clientele per move. I have found that
percentage to be a constant even when the
move is done correctly and professionally.
That percentage will increase if the move is
not executed well, if the relocation is done
under duress, or if it seems sudden to your clientele base. You must take that loss of clientele into consideration if you feel relocation
will be necessary to obtain a rental position.
Do the math and factor that number into your
calculations when you consider your weekly
rental net income. The last thing you want is

to realize that you should have waited and built your clientele longer before you made a move.

Don't forget that the old saying "fortune favors the bold" is still true today. But fortune doesn't favor the stupid or the emotional. Make all of your decisions based on business principles.

Fashion Shows

Everyone loves a good show; in the world of beauty and glamour, the greatest shows on earth are fashion shows. Participating in fashion shows is an excellent way to recruit new clients and to maintain your motivation. Regrettably, most hairdressers avoid these kinds of events for a variety of reasons. Perhaps the greatest deterrent is the fear that fashion shows are difficult and expensive to produce. Nothing could be farther from the truth! Fashion shows do not have to be expensive, and they are relatively easy to promote.

Staging a successful fashion show requires a location that can accommodate a decent amount of people. The most successful shows I have been involved in were held at small nightclubs. Fashion shows held at nightclubs attract an adult audience of people who are concerned about their physical appearances. These potential clients also have a disposable income and are receptive to fashion-show entertainment. Furthermore, nightclub managers recognize the drawing power of these types of events and are therefore very willing to participate—especially if they don't have to do anything.

The arena. Visit a local popular club and talk to the promotions coordinator or the manager. Tell the manager what you have in mind and be certain to point out that the show will last no more than fifteen or twenty minutes. If the event lasts any longer than that, it will be considered a distraction from the club's normal business routine. You will also want promotional assistance from the club's DJ during the show. Ask the DJ to announce the show before it begins and use him during the event for drawings, announcements, and other activities. Book your event during the middle of the week. Nightclubs usually do not need extra business on Friday or Saturday evenings. But if you are allowed to stage a show on a weekend night, do it! Allow four or five weeks to put the fashion show together, and use the following guidelines for success.

Get help. Ask two or three hairdressers from your salon to participate with you. Do not invite stylists from other salons, even if those stylists are your friends. In the end, you want all of the new business to come to one place. When more than one salon is competing for attention, it always gets ugly—trust me. You can do a show by yourself, but the added help will greatly increase your chance of success. You will appreciate the extra help, and the other stylists will appreciate the new business. Next decide on the number of models you want to use. If you are doing the show alone, I recommend using no more than twelve models. To use more would be a significant burden on you; remember that you will have to style each model the evening of the show. With the assistance of other hairdressers, you can work with twenty or more models; but remember that you should not sacrifice quality for quantity.

Select your models. First you should look for models by reviewing your clientele list. Clients who are chosen to model will always be more reliable than models you know through a casual association. Your clients will always be more reliable because they will already have a relationship with you. Your own clients will love the idea of being selected and will feel more loyal to you because of it. If you cannot find enough models from your clientele lists, consider using friends and family. If you still need additional models, get aggressive and go to a neighboring mall, college, or nightspot to recruit them. Remember that strangers don't have any relationship with you and will always be more likely to let you down.

Make sure you have some say in how your models dress. Splashy sex appeal for the night of the show is always good. Your models should look better than the regular customers in the nightclub. The simple fact is that sex sells, particularly in a nightclub setting—but avoid sleaziness. Models should still look classy. The audience should be left with the impression that you are a professional with style and class. The feel and look of the show need not and should not necessarily reflect your personal morals or convictions. The show is simply a show—a product—and you earn a living by marketing your skills and getting your name out there.

Decide on a format for the show. Do you want models to walk out two by two? Is the fashion show going to have a costume or hair theme? Will the models move through the audience, or will they stop and pose? Use your imagination and talk to the other stylists to get their input. Remember that there aren't any rules. You can format your show however you'd like. Your one objective is to create something exciting and tasteful that will make the average person want to look like the models you have styled. Above all, you want to be viewed as a professional. Your goal is to attract new clients. Keep that in mind.

If necessary, ask a local clothing apparel store to feature and furnish the outfits for your models. Smaller boutiques will usually jump at the chance to dress the models and promote their businesses. You might even talk them into donating a gift certificate that you can raffle off the night of the show. If you work with a company to dress your models, make certain that you advertise the store and give them credit throughout the show. However, you need to remember that if the clothing is damaged, you may be liable for replacement costs. To avoid liability, get the store involved in staging the fashion show and let them assume costs related to damage.

Finishing details. Pay attention to the little things that will make the fashion show a success. Choose and prepare your own music. Ask the DJ for his assistance with music playback. If your show is even a little bit choreographed, you will have to rehearse. Logistically, it may be hard to get everyone together to rehearse. Make a fun night of it a week before the show. Ask the salon owner if you can use the salon after hours, and bring in some pizza and snacks if you'd like. The point is that you only have one chance to make a first impression on the crowd. Make it a good one.

Don't forget to promote. The only goal of the fashion show is to attract new clientele. If you concentrate on the show and forget to get new business out of it, what's the point? Place business cards on each table just before the show starts—you need to advertise. The club manager should agree to this minor request. Provide the models with audience pleasers like small gifts that can be tossed out into the crowd. I've used lollipops with business cards attached, which works very well. There is something about a pretty girl throwing something into the air—it gets everyone's attention.

Talk to your current retail product vendors. Ask them for product samples that you can give away. You can also ask them for some full-sized products that you can raffle off. Put some plastic around any two or three products to make a great basket raffle prize. Call every vendor you deal with and let them know you will promote their products on the night of the show. Remember that if you don't ask, you don't get. Don't forget to put your business card on everything! Hold drawings at the end, offering gift certificates for free haircuts. Place pens and a stack of cards asking for names, addresses, and e-mail addresses on each table. Have the DJ announce the drawings and ask customers to complete and return the information cards to a central location if they want to be included in the drawing. Or, have one of your more outgoing models walk around and remind people to fill them out. At the time of the drawing, pick four or five female names from the cards. I know it sounds bad to only choose the females, but they will be your clients and the ones who will create excitement about you. When it comes time to announce the drawing, coordinate with the DJ beforehand and make sure he lets you announce the winners. Keep each information card that was turned in and do a discount mailer on a future date. If you or the salon have a business—not personal—Facebook page, find a way to get that information out there so people can follow you.

Remember that this is your fashion show. Capitalize on it by creating excitement. I once strapped small flashlights to the knees of my models and had them walk out to a dark stage during the show opener. The sky is the limit. Just remember why you are there.

Don't forget about the men. Make sure you plan your show so that it will please everyone. The beautiful women who model for you will make the men happy, but the bulk of your new clients will be women, so take care of the women in the crowd, too. I always had a few good-looking guys model for me, too. It mixes things up and keeps the women interested. Maybe you could check with the local fire department and ask if a few of the younger good-looking firefighters would consider modeling. If you throw a couple of firefighters out there, you will fire up the women for sure.

The club will judge your success based on the attendance and the number of drinks sold during the show. Realize this, and make sure to promote the event through social networking sites and any other outlet you can think of—especially if you want to return to do another show again.

Hairdressers have staged fashion shows at nightclubs before. However, many of them lose sight of their objective. Their natural tendency is to be artistic. For industry trade shows, artistry is your objective. However, at nightclubs you only have fifteen or twenty minutes to put on a show that will entertain your audience. Frankly, nightclub customers are not at all interested in watching you perform your skill. They want entertainment. So give it to them. They need to know who you are, but they want to see the show.

Do exciting work on your models, but give the nightclub customers entertainment, music, beautiful models, glitz, and action, and advertise the nightclub. If you succeed at this, the customers will remember your name.

The Biyearly Builder

The best way to build business is to advertise through your clientele. Word-of-mouth advertising is the beauty industry's most powerful promotional resource. If you want to be successful, you must use this resource extensively and intentionally.

How do you turn an existing client into a promotional tool? The answer is actually quite simple: change. Keep clients interested in you and their appearance by promoting periodic makeovers. Boredom with their appearance is the main reason clients stop referring new customers to a hairdresser. It is also the main reason why clients leave to find a new hairdresser.

Think back to when you first started your career as a hairdresser. At that time, you intentionally set out to build a clientele base. Your primary motivation was economic survival. You were charged with the excitement of entering into a new profession and building a base of regular customers. Clients sensed your love for the game and made repeated referrals to friends and coworkers. If it's a different situation now, why is that? You must recapture the motivation and excitement of those early days and share it with your clients. To that end, I developed the "biyearly builder."

The biyearly builder is a simple concept. It will help you to excite your existing clientele base by suggesting new looks to them, and it will get your clients to aggressively refer new customers to you again. To implement this program, simply mark off a six-week period on your calendar. During this time, you will commit to giving each and every client that sits in your chair two new ideas for his or her hair. Now you might be thinking that you can't think of that many new ideas for all of those people. Yes, you can. If you have one hundred people with appointments in that six-week period, you don't have to think of two hundred original ideas. All you need to do is think of two new ideas for the guests in your chair—take it one person at a time. If the two ideas you come up with for your second guest of the day are similar to the two you suggested to your first guest of the day, that's OK. They just need to be new for the person in your chair. (Review your client files and make sure you aren't suggesting a look that you just moved your guest out of on her last appointment.)

The crucial point to understand is that you need to infect clients with the excitement and promise of a new look. Except for a little nudge and subtle stroke to the ego, don't push the new ideas. Merely suggesting the change is enough. It is not necessary for your clients to accept your recommendations. In my experience with implementing this program for many years, only about half of your guests will actually say, "That sounds great—do that today." The important thing is that you plant the seed of the idea. Planting the seed of a new idea is money in the bank for a hairdresser who is bent on success. Some people need some time to think new ideas over. They aren't able to be that spontaneous, and that's OK. After implementing this program, a large number of your clients will remember the new idea you gave them on their last visit and ask you if you will do it during their next visit. Remember that some of the new ideas will be for a chemical or color change. On the day you suggest the new idea, you might only have the guest scheduled for a forty-five-minute haircut and style and won't actually have the time to give her the new color you just suggested. That's all right. If she likes the idea, set that new service up on the way out as you prebook her next appointment. That way, she will have five or six weeks to become excited about it and to tell her friends what you're going to do for her.

This brings us to the second crucial point you need to understand: Promoting change is a sign of motivation, and motivation is a sign of professional interest. If your clients get the sense that you are not interested in what you do or have lost interest in it, they will lose interest in you. When a regular or repeat client sits down in your chair, *never* assume you will be doing the same thing you did the last time. If your guest wants you to do the same thing you did for her last appointment, it should always be her idea. If you ever hear yourself ask if a style worked out OK last time and if she just wants you to clean it up again, walk into the restroom, slap yourself in the face, and start again. When you assume you are doing the same thing that you did during the last appointment, you seem like a burnt-out hairdresser. Don't be that person.

As I said before, a number of clients will ask you to give them the new change on the spot. Some will have to think about it. Some will have to wait until you have ample time to give it to them. Regardless, the result will be the same; your clientele base will know you are someone who is excited about what he or she does. They will know you are someone they can feel good about referring their friends to, because their friends will have the same experience that they had. They will know you are someone who is always considering new ways to make them feel and look more attractive. When you're clients are talking about you, new people will book consultations with you. Consultations equal appointments. Appointments equal more referrals and consultations. Get the picture?

Implement the biyearly builder while you are doing your normal consultation with your guest. Before the shampoo, let her know that you have been thinking of some new ideas for her. If you have some example photos, show them to her. If there is any way to help her visualize your idea, make it easy for her to see the picture you have in your mind. Above all, make the consultation personal. The guest should feel as if you are thinking of this change for her alone. Be excited about your suggestions, and your guest will get excited, too. Never tell your clients that you are implementing a client-building program. They should feel as if you have just thought of this great new idea and you had to share it with them.

Only implement the biyearly builder once every six months. If you promote change more often, clients may think you are uncertain about what looks best on them. If you actively promote change every six months, they will simply think of you as someone who is always on top of style changes and will always keep them up to date.

Let's say you have sixty regular clients. You will see each one of those clients within the six-week biyearly builder. Out of the sixty clients you service, maybe 15 percent will recommend you to a friend or coworker. So at the end of your biyearly builder, you will have a total of sixty-nine clients in your base. Six months later, it will be time for you to implement the biyearly builder again. If 15 percent of your clients refer someone to you, you will have a clientele base of eighty clients. You can do the math from there. This is a numbers game. As long as you stay consistent, the more people you do this with, the more new clients you will have. It's that simple.

I started implementing this program because I found it difficult to continually come up with new ideas for every guest and to stay motivated all of the time. Putting this six-week period on my calendar twice a year helped me make sure that I stayed current with my ideas and didn't do the same thing all the time. It forced me stay motivated and pushed me to remain creative. This is the most successful business-building program I have developed. This program alone will keep you motivated and current. Most importantly, it will prevent you from becoming like the rest of the hair stylists out there.

Doing this program is like having a friend drag you to the gym. You can see it on the calendar, you know your friend is coming over, and you're going to have to go.

Competition

In the beauty industry, establishing a reputation and setting yourself above the crowd is essential. One of the best ways to do that is to participate in in trade-show competitions.

I competed in my first hair show while I was still in beauty school. I was in my freshman class and had only 180 hours of classroom training behind me. I competed in a small trade show in Riverside, California. I competed in a haircut-and-style competition. I took third place out of twenty-five competitors and received a small trophy and a check for twenty-five dollars. On the advice of my mentor, Johnny Hernandez, I took the trophy to school the next day and put it right on top of my workstation where everyone could see it. I also put a couple of before-and-after photos up so people could get an idea of what I had done. The vast majority of the students in my class resented me, and that startled me. It was then that I realized I was on the road to separating myself from my peers. I liked it. Johnny told me that you know you're on the right track when they all start to hate you. Think about it. If your goal in this business is to be in the top 1 or 2 percent of income earners, will you be popular?

Doing that one competition was like getting a shot in the arm. It gave me a tremendous amount of confidence and established that I could and would be different from the thousands of hairdressers out there. If you decide to compete, do not be concerned with taking home trophies. It was not the trophy that gave me confidence. My confidence came from putting aside my fear about competing professionally in public. Competing and winning is great, but winning isn't necessary to set yourself apart from your peers. The fact that you are part of the small percentage of people who aren't afraid to show what they can do in public will set you apart. If you place or win, it's just a bonus. You need to throw away all of your doubt and worries about what people may think. You will be scared to death initially, but once you start working on your model, all of those feelings will go away. I promise that after you compete for your first time, you will never feel that way again. The confidence you will have and the energy it will give you will become addictive, and you won't be able to wait until the next competition.

From a business standpoint, competition is a great way to establish a reputation and generate client interest. Clients love to tell friends, family, and associates that their hairdresser is a show competitor. Do you personally know any hairdressers who compete? Most don't, and that's the point. Are you with the pack or leading it? As I stated earlier, winning isn't necessary. Simply competing makes you different from others. Whether you win or lose, you should bring in plenty of pictures to show your clients. Talk about it, and tell them what it was like. This is a corner of the hair industry that very few clients have even heard of. They will love to hear about it, and the more they realize how few hairdressers participate, the more it will benefit you.

If you do bring home a trophy, don't be shy about promoting yourself. Bring it into work, display it on your workstation, and talk up your achievement. Make sure you have plenty of pictures to show your guests. Put the photos up on your Facebook page. I do this with every trophy I win, whether it is for first, second, or third place; each trophy has resulted in a significant increase in my customer base. Competition creates talk, and talk leads to new referrals.

Don't be surprised if your coworkers resent you. That is normal and should be expected. Resist the urge to be mad at them and to react negatively to their attitude toward you. It will not serve you well. Instead, encourage them to join you at the next competition.

I challenge you to compete in just one trade show to see what it does for your attitude, confidence, and business. I guarantee that it will renew your satisfaction in your career choice.

Hair-Care Maintenance and Retail Product Sales

You've just spent the last couple of hours carefully coloring and shaping your client's hair. She's happy; you're happy. Now it's time to move on to the next guest. Or is it?

Service does not end at the moment you pre-book a client for her next appointment. You have an obligation—and hopefully a personal commitment—to provide your clients with the necessary tools to maintain their hair in between appointments. These tools are the professional-quality hair-care products you use and sell in your salon.

Try this simple exercise. The next time you give a haircut to one of your fellow stylists or family members, do not use any styling products on them at all. From the beginning to the end, use nothing. Now consider this: You're very good at doing hair. You're better at doing hair than your clients are. That's why they come to you. If you can't finish a style and make it look great without a product of any kind, how do you expect your clients to be able to make their hair look great without retail products at home? This concept needs to be burned into your head, and you need to make this idea the main reason for recommending products for your guests to purchase.

Selling retail products is an important tool that can help you successfully build a clientele base. It provides your customers with a home product that will help them duplicate what you have done at the salon. I go so far as to say my to clients, "I'm pretty good at this, and I can't make your hair look this way without these products. If you like what I have done, you will need these products to duplicate this style." Your clients will understand that and will appreciate your honesty, even if they resent the fact that they must spend more money on products.

Why do hairdressers use professional hair-care products? Quite simply, they provide superior care for the clients' hair. It makes sense, then, to encourage our clientele to take the same products home with them. The reason you don't use lower-quality/lower-cost products from the drug store is because they don't work as well and you don't get the same end result. The same will be true for your clients. It's sort of like buying a beautiful new Ferrari. Do you spend all that money just to put cheap fuel in it? It may run if you do, but it not like it was designed to run. If your guests use lower-quality products on their hair, they will be frustrated with their results and with their inability to duplicate the salon look—it's that simple. If she cannot maintain the style you gave her in the salon, then she will not receive compliments on her hair, and you will not be likely to get her friends and associates as referral customers. Customers know that the salon products you use are several grades above the retail hair-care products they buy at local supermarkets and drugstores. The results that come with using quality products will be obvious to them the moment they see you put the final touches on their hair. You need to capitalize on this important observation—you need to promote your products for take-home use. In fact, you have a professional obligation to advise clients on the importance of using the products you recommend. If they trust you to suggest a new color or a cut change, they will trust you when it comes to duplicating and maintaining their style.

You must have the confidence to make this subject seem important. I say "confidence" because of all the subjects I discuss in this book;

the subject of retail sales seems to bother stylists more than any other. Stylists want to be creative and artistic, and they don't want to sell. I couldn't agree more. I never sell retail product. I merely educate my clients. *I don't sell—I tell.* It sounds like a catchy little phrase, but it's true. If you change your thought process and view selling products as being professional and educating your clients, the products will sell themselves.

If your client is using inferior products at home, it's safe to assume that she will receive inferior results when she styles her hair. As stylists, we understand this. But consider this: For years, your clientele base has been bombarded with advertising telling them that the products they buy at the supermarket are amazing and wonderful for their hair. The models in those advertisements are beautiful, and their hair is stunning. Let me share a true fact with you that I've learned from personal experience: If you don't educate your clients about the differences between what they see in television ads and the products you recommend at the salon, your clients will blame you for their results. It's not fair, but it will happen.

The proliferation of beauty supply stores has significantly increased your competition. However, you have two advantages over retail outlets: Your clients represent an instant and loyal base of retail product customers, and they trust your recommendations for hair-care products. Your clients come to you for a professional service and professional advice. Some stylists give the service but forget to give the advice. Your clients want and deserve both from you. We are in one of the few industries that allow professionals to promote and sell the products we use during the course of our services. It gives us an extra measure of credibility with our clients.

Let me share a simple concept with you. It's called "CYA," or cover your a———! This concept is especially important when it comes to color, chemical treatments, and retail product sales. The process of doing hair is pretty simple. When it comes to color, we are introducing artificial pigment molecules into the hair, and we want them to stay there for as long as possible. Some conditions help those molecules stay longer, and some conditions make those molecules slip out faster. It's that simple. You will get the credit for how that process ends up working out for your client regardless of whether it works out well or poorly. If you are not brave enough to be honest with your clients and to be a true professional, you will suffer for it, and your income will suffer for it, too.

In the beginning of my career, I tried to be everything to everyone. I wanted to make everyone as happy as possible. When a client had a difficult time with the extra cost of the product she needed to take home, I told her not to worry about it and said maybe she could get it next time. I was more concerned with filling my appointment book than I was with selling products. I didn't understand that everything is connected and that by not standing firm and being honest with my clients, I was shooting myself in the foot. I soon realized that when a new color service faded very quickly or when a client received a negative comment about the awkward shade of her color, I was to blame, even though the fading was due to the drugstore product she had used. I saw it affect my referral rate and, ultimately, my income in general. I made the decision then to be brave and honest with my clients. In fact, I would set a standard for the way I did business when it came to retail product sales.

This is what I did: Each time I did a consultation for a color or chemical service, I told the guest that I would not guarantee the results or longevity of the service unless she took home the products I recommended to her. I told the guest that it was not an attempt to promote sales. After giving my clients a basic education about hair physiology and what my products, as opposed to inferior products, did, I assured them I was merely treating them with professional respect and letting them know what they needed. I then gave them an example and said, "When you go for a doctor's appointment, you doctor prescribes what you need based on your condition. It's the same with your hair. This is what you need. You don't have to buy it, but I won't be held responsible for the results if you choose not to use it." That meant that I would not redo a color that faded prematurely as I had done in the past.

Taking this stance with my clients was a bit scary at first, but when I did, the results were amazing. It yielded a windfall of positive effects. The loyalty of my clientele base seemed to increase overnight. All of my chemical services looked better and stayed that way longer. My clients seemed to respect me more for my honesty. Knowing I was doing the right thing for my clients and that I wasn't spending my time recoloring clients who had faded their own hair made me feel more professional. All it took was a bit of bravery on my part, and I never looked back.

I'm sure that some people didn't like this policy of mine. I'm sure that I didn't make everyone happy. That's OK. In the end, you can only be professional and do what is best for your clients. Don't be afraid to stick to a policy that you know is right and makes the most business sense.

Don't forget that every detail of the service we give our clients is connected to either a positive or a negative outcome. Just because everything in this book is broken down into individual subjects doesn't mean that you can cherry-pick and choose the things you want to do or feel comfortable with. It is all one process, and everything is connected. You have to do everything if you want to succeed. Everything counts in the big picture.

The Psychology of Building Client Loyalty

Building loyalty—it's a phrase I use liberally throughout this manual. If you don't build loyalty with your clients, you will never succeed as a hairdresser. The concept of building loyalty is that important.

Before we go on, can we first agree that loyalty is essential to a successful clientele base? It's up there with the concept of trust. I am purposely not going to write on this subject and instead will leave it as a fact. If I have to convince you that the loyalty of your clientele is important, please put this book down, because you're wasting your time.

Hairdressers employ a number of approaches to build a loyal clientele base. Most achieve only average results. I, too, have utilized a number of concepts for building loyalty. Of these, one stands out above the rest. It employs a basic social concept called "gratitude." In practice, it is the deliberate and conscious effort to encourage clients to build a personal attachment with you. It is achieved through a simple offering of a gift. The gift, by the way, is not for your client. The gift is for you! Earning the gratitude of your clients is not difficult at all. The first step is to establish trust, and I am here to tell you that trust is something you gained the moment the guest first sat in your chair. You have to own this idea and have confidence in it. To understand what I mean, you need to understand the psychological concept of "personal zones."

I want to tell you about the psychology of personal zones. As hairdressers, we are neither priests nor counselors nor psychologists; nonetheless, we all of play these roles to one degree or another throughout the course of our careers. Clients relax under our care—they trust us and want to confide in us. Customers will also confide in a local bartender, right? The defining difference between a hairdresser and a local bartender is touch. There is something about human contact that makes people open up to us more. That one factor makes our industry so satisfying—we really get to know the people whom we take care of. It also gives us an amazing opportunity to connect with our guests. A client who shares a personal story or a "secret" with you (either intentionally or unintentionally) is establishing a personal social bond with you. These bonds need to be deliberately and intentionally encouraged, and they will establish loyalty to you as a person and not just as a hairdresser.

Why do guests feel comfortable telling secrets to their hairdressers? The answer lies in the intimacy associated with touching someone's hair. It's the human touch, and that touch requires them to trust us.

The brain is the controlling organ of the body, and it is without question the body's most important organ. Most people establish what psychologists label a "personal zone" around their heads to protect their brains and to ward off unwanted aggressors. Freely and repeatedly encroaching upon the personal zone is the essence of power. This pattern of invasion is reserved for a person's most intimate associates. Our clients grant us license to enter their personal zones, and that trust can serve as a primary tool for building a loyal clientele. This may sound a bit heavy to some, but think about it. Itit makes perfect sense. As I have said many times already, successfully very little about building a clientele has very little to do with physically doing hair. It's all about how people feel, and not just how they look. It's about learning the psychology of the trade. Your objective is to encourage the guest to build a personal and professional attachment to you—that is the basis of building loyalty. It is essential that you maintain a business relationship, but she should have an opportunity to occasionally express her feelings in a personal way. There is a fine line between affording this opportunity to clients and taking advantage of it as a hairdresser. I will discuss this more in depth in the chapter called "Professional Distance." For me, the way to achieve this is to allow the clients opportunities to show gratitude.

Accepting Client Gratitude. During the Christmas season, for example, I have seen many hairdressers order promotional items from their salon's product representatives. These items are ordered as gifts for clients as a token of appreciation for returning year after year. I get it. I understand the idea. Those hairdressers' hearts are in the right place; but their approach is backwards. I simply feel it's counter productive and sending the wrong message. Keep one thing in mind, however, that these clients are returning year after year for one main reason—YOU.

During the course of each year and each appointment, you showed demonstrate your skills to of enhancing the natural beauty of your clients; —in some cases the assignment has is not always been easy. You make special arrangements to squeeze a guest in at the last moment. You stayed after normal work hours for a client who is running late or for who has a special occasion. You searched for special products to satisfy a client's particular needs. You set aside time at home with family and friends to be available to guests for special occasions like weddings, graduations, birthdays, and anniversaries. You give loyal clients the gift of free services for those special moments in their lives.

The gift is in the giving, and you give throughout the year. You have done your work, and you have built a loyal following. It is now essential that you permit each client to demonstrate his or her loyalty to you. Your task is simple: you need to allow clients to give to you, but you also need to encourage that action in a way that does not threaten, demand, or show expectations. I learned a simple truth years ago and have shared this truth with my staff many times. You have hundreds of clients, and they only have one of you. You must "own" this attitude, but never with arrogance. It is simply a fact of the business, and we must act accordingly. To accomplish this, we use a simple tool—humor.

Clients wonder if it's appropriate to bring you gifts. The answer is yes. A gift is no different from the tip you receive after each appointment—it is simply more personal. That's a good thing, as long as it's coming from your client! Give your clients the opportunity to bring you gifts they choose. Do not discourage it. Remember that you want your clients to think of you when they are away from the salon. You want to be in a different category in their lives. If you are lumped together in the same group as a client's dentist, doctor, and attorney, you can be easily replaced. It's hard for people to replace someone who is close to them. You need to encourage that closeness. This is simply an easy way to do that without crossing the line of professionalism. This concept is all about changing your mind-set. Remember that your guests want to appreciate you. Remember the concept of "personal zones."

Let me give a few examples of how this has worked for me in the past and how I have used this concept effectively and still managed to keep things professional.

> **Your birthday**. Each year when my birthday is approaching, I use the opportunity to plant the seed of the idea that a gift might be in order. Again, this is done

with humor, never with an expectation of a gift, and never in a way that makes a guest feel it's required. Humor—plant the seed. When prebooking a client's next appointment, I would say something like, "You know, that appointment is pretty close to my birthday, just so you know." Then I would laugh. Or I might say, "Your next appointment will fall a few weeks after my birthday. I'm letting everyone know that I'll be accepting gifts sixty days after my birthday, just to make it convenient." Laugh—it's a joke. (Or is it?) At the least, you client will get a laugh and feel you are connecting with her on a personal level. She will also walk away wondering if she's supposed to give her hairdresser a gift on his or her birthday. That's a good thing. The seed is planted.

Christmas. A big holiday is the same idea. When your guest is on the way out and you're prebooking her next appointment, jokingly inquire whether she has budgeted for your Christmas gift. Does she need any ideas? Tell her you're registered at Tiffany's. Again, be funny, and use humor! Chances are good that you won't end up with an expensive piece of jewelry. More likely you'll receive a nice gift card to a local coffeehouse. Terrific!

Everyday occasions. If a client calls in to say that she is running late for a scheduled appointment, let her know that she is still fine. Ask her to pick you up a coffee on the way to the salon if she happens to see a Starbucks. If a guest asks if you can stay late to fit in a color service at the end of a haircut appointment, suggest she stop and pick you both up some food on the way in because you'll be missing dinner. You get the idea. This is a simple but very effective way to allow your clients to connect with you on a personal level. That is what this exercise is all about. Don't be afraid. This is done with humor so as to not make someone feel obligated to do something, and it is done with confidence, not arrogance!

Do not be shy about accepting a gift. You are doing this intentionally and for a specific purpose. It's OK to be a little bold about the whole thing. Here is a good example of that. My mentor and business partner, Johnny Hernandez, worked with me for many years. He is the person who taught me this concept and showed me how to use it correctly. We had an understanding between us regarding gifts from clients. The understanding was that we would help each other because we knew how important this was to building our business. When a client came in and gave me a gift of some kind—even a cup of coffee—I would turn to Johnny and say very loudly, "Hey Johnny, what did your client bring you today? Cindy brought me a nice hot cup of coffee." Johnny knew the drill, and he would immediately turn to the client in his chair and say, "Why didn't you bring me coffee today?" He would do it with humor, not with expectation. But he planted the seed of the idea of gratitude with his client. My client felt good because she was recognized (loudly and sort of embarrassingly) for her gift—she felt special. When Johnny had a client who brought him something, the roles and the script were reversed. The intention of the game and the little comedy act was to "shame" our clients for not thinking of bringing us something that day. It was always funny and never serious, but it was always effective.

The gift is not the point. The point is that you are in a different category in your client's life. You're in the category of people she presents personal gifts to. A relationship built strictly on business is easily broken. A relationship built on the bonds of loyalty and friendship is long lasting. That is the point.

Upselling Your Services

Each time a guest sits in your chair for a service, you should immediately think "upsell." Upselling is when you offer an additional service on top of the one you've already agreed upon. A classic example of an upsell comes to us from the fast-food industry: Every customer placing a food order receives an upsell pitch when the employee behind the counter asks, "Do you want fries with that order?"

Upselling is a promotional business practice that you need to become familiar with and a skill you have to get good at if you expect to see your business flourish. However, unlike in the fast-food example above, hairdressers should offer upsells only when they can provide a service that is truly beneficial to their guests. If you do it strictly for profit, you have crossed the line.

The upsell does not need to be complicated. It should not feel like a sale at all. If it feels like that to you, change the way you present it.

An upsell should be nothing more than an idea you give and a simple way to suggest an extra service that might not have crossed the mind of your guest. Let me give a working example. A regular client comes in for a makeover after building up the courage to go for that big change. As you do the consultation and discuss what she would like, you see one more change that would complete the "look." Maybe it's just a few foils of color in a specific area. Simply suggest it. Don't worry if she passes on your suggestion. The point is to plant the seed of the idea of the service. If your guest takes advantage of your suggestion right then and there, that's terrific. If she passes on the suggestion, there is a good chance she will think about having it done on her next appointment. Either way, you have put the idea of an extra service into her head. That's the idea.

Many stylists are very shy about suggesting more services to their guests. They feel that their clients are already spending enough on their appointments. They feel that they know what their clients can afford. They are worried they will be viewed as someone who is just trying to get more money off of their clientele. I am going to be very blunt on this matter— that is the thinking of a loser! That is the sort of thinking that will keep people making less than twenty-five thousand dollars a year in this amazing industry. Just like many of the concepts in this book, the success of this concept depends on how it is done. I don't know anyone in this industry who wants to be viewed as or feel like a salesperson. I am no exception to that rule. That is why I will never sell a thing to anyone, and I would never encourage you to sell, either. But you can upsell your services without selling. All you need to do is tell your guests what you think and describe how you feel about the idea. Be excited and animated when you describe your idea. If you're excited, chances are good that they will be excited about the idea, too. Don't sell—tell.

The upsell works very much the same as an impulse buy works, which makes it a particularly powerful tool for building your business. Think about the number of times you have been in the grocery store and picked up a pack of gum as you passed through the checkout simply because you saw it there. That is an impulse buy. People like to be spontaneous. Make this principle work for you. With your friends and family, practice different ways to put these ideas across to your clients. Ask for their feedback about which approaches makes them feel less pressured, less like they're being sold something, and more likely to say "yes." This is a skill that you need to get good at. It is not something that comes naturally to anyone. That is why you need to practice it and role-play with friends and family. You need to know which approach makes people feel the best and gets the best response from you clientele.

One of the biggest obstacles to success in the hair business is simply getting over fear— fear of being viewed in a certain light, fear of embarrassment, and fear of what other stylists will think. Think about your life growing up. Something is only scary when you have no experience with it. Once you know what something is and what it will do, you're not afraid of it any longer. And if you have success at something that you were afraid of, the fear goes away.

This concept, like many others in this book, will work that same way. You have to just do it! For years, I have told my staff to simply "fake it till you make it." Pretend a concept doesn't scare you until it doesn't any longer. But do it! If you're afraid to recommend additional services, how are you going to have the nerve to recommend the hair-care products your guests need after that amazing color? For example, say your client just spent over two hundred dollars on color services and a haircut. She needs good products to take home with her. If she doesn't take them home, her color will fade. What will you do? Will you only recommend a product to someone if he or she spends under two hundred dollars on a service? Will you prejudge a client and decide if she can afford the product or service that you know she needs? If you do, you will lose this game, my friend. You must commit yourself to a standard of doing business. You must have a system that you follow, and you must execute that system with each and every client you service—no exceptions.

The weakest link in many businesses is, unfortunately, the person running the business. Don't be that person. Be consistent. Be deliberate. Be intentional. In the hair business, you will truly be the person who makes you or breaks you. You will never be able to blame your failure or success on anyone else. Make your decisions, and be consistent.

The "Killer" Shampoo

It is known as the "killer" shampoo—the touch that gets them talking and the touch that brings them back. You learned about it in beauty school. Remember the elderly women who always came in for the shampoo and set? Remember how they encouraged you to "scrub harder, honey"? Listen to the wisdom of age. Those ladies know that if the shampoo is not the only reason for visiting a hairdresser, it sure is a big part of it. Yes, they want their hair done, but if the shampoo were not "killer," they would ask for a different stylist on their next visit.

What is the secret to giving a "killer shampoo"? Massage! I know this is a simple concept, but think about how many times you might have been running a little behind on your schedule and brought your next client back to you chair quickly at the expense of her/his "killer" shampoo. I would say we have all done it once or twice. Think about getting a pedicure. You want your toenails to look good; however, if a foot massage weren't included, the pedicure would not be complete and you probably would not return.

There is a small salon in Southern California that made their shampoo the cornerstone of any service they provided. It was so important that they created a separate room with specific lighting, music, aroma, and colors for the shampoo area. The shampoo experience would literally take up to twenty minutes or more of each service. In a matter of weeks, they were booked night and day. Word quickly got around that there was a very enjoyable and relaxing aspect to every service the salon provided. They continue to be very successful today.

The point is that the shampoo is nothing to take for granted and is about the only opportunity we have to physically connect with a client in a pleasurable way. That can be a very powerful tool when it's used, and it's a very powerful tool to waste.

Establish a standard policy of giving a killer shampoo to everyone who comes in for a service with you, regardless of whether your clients are men or women. The whole process should never take more than ten minutes or less than five minutes. When you take the right amount of time to give a correct shampoo, the experience will result in a life-time client.

Before you shampoo a guest's hair, ask if she would like a complimentary scalp treatment. Don't use the word "massage." For many people, "massage" implies intimacy, which may cause your guests to feel uncomfort-able. "Scalp treatment" is a clinical term that means the same thing as "massage."

After completing the shampoo, add condi-tioner to the hair. Use the conditioner as a lubri-cant for performing the scalp treatment/mas-sage. Conditioner reduces friction between your hands and your guest's hair and scalp. Do not talk while performing your scalp treat-ment. This should be a moment or relaxation for your guest. If your client asks about the ther-apeutic advantages of the scalp treatment, be prepared to educate her. Tell her that the treatment increases blood flow to the scalp, which in turn feeds and stimulates the hair follicles. When you massage an area, blood rushes there. (That's why your hair grows more in warm weather. Your blood is thinner when it's warm like it is in the summertime, and that means increased blood flow to everywhere, including to your hair.)

If you are working with an assistant or an intern and are almost ready for your next guest, have your assistant or intern perform the killer shampoo ten minutes before you are finished with your current guest. Showing your next guest attention early on in the process is impressive, and it will help you make sure that she gets her full shampoo experience and you stay on schedule.

The following tip is about something special for your male clients. If you have a clientele already, you already know that men tend to be very loyal. Do not take that fact for granted for a minute. Give your male guests something special when they come in.   W h e n you are about to shampoo a man, ask him if he would like a complimentary hot towel on his face with his shampoo. Always ask first because some people feel claustrophobic when something is covering their face, and you want this to be a pleasurable experience.

First, lean the gentleman back into the shampoo bowl. Get some hot water running in the bottom of the bowl. When the water is good and hot, take a clean white towel and completely soak it in the hot water. Turn off your water. Then use a shampoo that has either peppermint or eucalyptus oil in it (you can find them at most distributors) or something with a menthol scent to it. Put one full pump of shampoo onto the towel that is in the bottom of the bowl. Move the towel around in your hands to distribute the shampoo and wring out most of the water in the towel. Now it's time to put it on your guest's face. Let him know in advance that you're going to cover his mouth, but not his nose. First, though, you need to make sure the towel it not too hot. Open the towel and place it on his neck, chin, and mouth. Wrap the towel up along his face and cross it over his eyes and forehead. You can cover his mouth, but do not cover his nose. His nose is the only part of his face that you should see. Ask him if he is OK. If he is feeling claustrophobic, he will feel free to tell you.

Now start your normal shampoo, but make sure you use the same shampoo that you put into the towel. The whole shampoo and condition should be done while the towel is on his face. At the end of the shampoo, have another clean white towel in your hand when you slide the wet towel off of his face. Slide it down toward his chin to take it off. The clean white towel should go on his face as soon as the wet one comes off. Then you should blot his face dry; do not wipe his face. Wiping his face will ruin the whole experience for him.

It's too rough. Sit your guest up and ask him how it was. You will be surprised how much this small value-added service will add to the loyalty of your clientele. The whole process will take roughly five to seven minutes to complete. This service can obviously be done on women too, but most women will be wearing makeup and will not appreciate your altering it.

The Power of Humor

I attribute a good portion of my success in this business to the power of humor. I learned early on in my professional career that if a customer receives quality service and enjoys her service appointment, she is likely to return and become a loyal and referring customer. I make it a very serious rule to get at least one laugh out of each client before he or she leaves my chair. I feel so strongly about the benefits of humor and how it affects the total customer experience that getting at least one laugh out of my guest is high up on my "each-client" checklist of things that have to happen during the appointment.

Humor may not come easily to you; nonetheless, you should make it a priority. Developing humor as a skill will give you an enormous psychological advantage with your clients. Instead of waiting for this to happen by chance, why not make it a part of what you do with everyone who sits in your chair? Getting a laugh out of your guest should be on your list along with a good consultation, upselling ser-vices, selling retail products, and prebooking. It's just what happens every time. It's how you operate. Your clients will love your confidence and ease. People buy confidence more than they buy any other attribute. Maintaining an easy sense of humor while providing a profes-sional service screams confidence.

I speak at beauty/hair schools quite a bit. Whenever I speak on this subject, I always use the same example to try to drive home the importance of this point. I will choose two dif-ferent students on opposite sides of the room. I will ask them to stand and state their names. For argument's sake, let's say the names of these two students are Alexa and Nikki. I go through an overly dramatic account about how Alexa and Nikki both have about the same amount of school hours and experi-ence under their belts. Then I ask them to imagine that a client comes in one day for a haircut and sits down with Alexa. Alexa does a very nice haircut and style, and the client is very happy. Five weeks later, the same client comes back to the school and sits down with Nikki. Nikki does a very nice haircut and style too, and the client is happy again. But for some reason, the client laughed with Nikki. Who will the client choose for her third appointment five weeks from now? Sometimes the smallest bond is the deciding factor in a client's decision to select and remain with a hairdresser.

Laughter is a very powerful thing. It has medicinal value, promotes healing, and bonds people in subtle ways. I have a very simple philosophy. I believe that if a guest laughs with you, his or her appointment truly becomes a visit—and there is a big distinction between the two.

Most people have humorless days at work because the typical job environment offers little time to laugh. When clients come to your salon for services and see that you are eager to share a laugh, its sends a psychological message that you enjoy what you are doing and like your work. And as I stated earlier, it screams confidence.

Time for another example: Imagine you are sitting in the waiting area of a salon watching everyone work. You see two stylists working side by side. Both are doing beautiful work. Both seem very proficient and are very professional. But you notice that one seems to be a little on the quiet side. She is very serious. Perhaps she thinks it makes her appear more professional—who knows? The stylist next to her is not so quiet. She seems a bit more animated, and she and her client are laughing occasionally. They're having a good time. Which one of the stylists would seem more confident and sure of herself? Who would you rather sit down with?

Now it must be said that not every person likes this kind of personality. Some would choose the more serious stylist. In my experience, though, you will attract more people to you when you are at ease and demonstrate a bit of humor. Besides, I personally would rather have a clientele full of people who laugh than people who don't. The bond established when a client enjoys her visit is hard to measure. It is essential for you to make it obvious that you enjoy your work, and because humor is contagious, I suggest you share it.

The final lesson in this chapter is about how to build trust and loyalty with your clients. Establishing trust and loyalty with your clients is the only way to achieve success in this industry. You may have all the technical ability necessary to make a great hairdresser, but if you cannot establish trust and loyalty with your clientele, you will never successfully build a customer base. Humor can help this happen and must be consciously used for that purpose. Ask yourself this question: In the big picture, what is more important—the service you give your clients or how they feel when they leave?

When I speak on this subject, someone always asks, "What if I'm not naturally funny or don't have that kind of personality? What if humor doesn't come easily to me?" I always give the same answer: "You have to fake it till you make it." That means that you must get yourself out of your comfort zone and pretend that it is easy for you until it actually is. Consider all of the actors that we see on TV and in the movies. Very few of them were born with those acting abilities. Many of the actors we see are very shy people in real life. But they wanted to have a specific job, and they wanted to be successful at it. They knew they needed to get good at something that didn't come naturally to them if they wanted to make it and make a living at it. So they pretended until it came naturally to them. You can do that, too. All it takes is deliberate effort and determination. Haven't you ever heard someone say something like, "She is very shy most of the time, but when she dances in front of a crowd, she's a completely different person,"? That can be you, too. It doesn't have to be you—you just have to act that way.

Think of humor as a thread in the fabric that weaves a successful career in the hair industry. It is only one of many, but it is an important piece of thread.

The Chameleon Effect

Conversation. It is the glue between the hairdresser and the client. Without it, clients will drift away; monopolize it, and they will run away. Conversational skills are one of your most valuable assets. You must learn to use conversation to turn your captive audience into an admiring audience. Conversation establishes a connection that is not only important but is also absolutely necessary.

I am convinced that quality conversation is one of the main factors that a client considers when assessing a hair appointment as either pleasurable or disappointing. It is also the yardstick for evaluating how the two of you relate to each other. Each time you meet with a client, you are establishing a personal connection. This connection is largely related to how well you adapt yourself to suit the person in your chair. Just like a chameleon blends with its environment, you need to evaluate and understand the personality of your clients and adapt yourself to them. If you are not adapting to the personalities of your clients and giving them what they need, then you are using the appointment for yourself—and that's not good business. That is an error that I have very little patience for. Please forgive me in advance if I'm rather direct on the matter.   This industry is filled with hairdressers who use client appointments to satisfy their own needs. We have all seen it happen; a client sits down, and as soon as the service is decided upon, the stylist starts venting about her relationship, sex, the drama in the salon—you name it. To me, this is the height of ignorance, and it shows a lack of appreciation for one's clients. This industry deserves more from its members. When were we ever taught that it is OK and appropriate to monopolize a paying customer's time just because we are giving her a haircut? I will say this as plainly as I can: Hairdresser, it's not your appointment. The appointment belongs to the very nice woman who is paying for your time and putting up with your unprofessional attitude. Stop it now! You're giving us all a bad reputation.

I had to get that off my chest before I could talk about good conversation and how to create it. I needed you to pay attention to the polar opposite of good conversation and understand what we are not striving for so you could appreciate what we are working toward.

Knowing your clients. If I have a client who is a principal of a school and I want to engage her in a conversation related to education, what should I do? I don't have a background in education. Maybe I didn't even like school. The first and simplest way to engage a client in conversation is to ask questions. Ask them about their work. People like to talk about what they do and their experiences. You should always listen twice as much as you speak. As my grandfather used to say, "God gave you two ears and one mouth for a reason, son!" Do some reading. Find out basic information about general industries and how they work. Do a little homework from time to time so when you meet someone from an industry you know little about you can at least put together an intelligent question to get him or her talking. The obvious point is to gain some information about a broad spectrum of subjects. That way, you can appear knowledgeable about and interested in your clients' careers and what they have to say.

Talk about yourself if you choose, but do not do it on a consistent basis, and never do it during a first-time appointment. If you do, the client might regard you as egocentric and will probably not return for a second appointment. Let your clients find out about you in small doses over a long period of time. Remember that it's their time, not yours.

The intimidation factor. When it comes to conversation, some hairdressers are intimidated by clients in high-income brackets and have trouble relating to them. Do not be intimidated. The wealthy have egos, but they are no different from the rest of us. If you are not familiar with a wealthy client's profession, ask questions. If it seems like a client comes from "old money," ask about his or her family history. If your client comes from "new money," ask how he or she made his or her fortune. Get these people talking, but never let it seem like you are enamored of them. You are simply getting information and making conversation. Always remember that they are sitting in your chair and receiving a professional service that you are providing; you are always their equal. The wealthy like to talk; your only problem is staying awake during the conversation.

Improving your vocabulary. Your personal vocabulary is key to connecting with each client in your chair. If your vocabulary range is limited, you may have problems associating with clients from different professions, backgrounds, and income levels. Vocabulary development is essential for any professional climbing the ladder of success. Enriching your vocabulary is easy. You can do it by simply reading more. Pay attention to words you hear and words you read that you are not familiar with. Write those words down, look them up, and make a point to use them in conversation the next day. The publication Reader's Digest has a section called "Improving Your Word Power," and it will help you do just that.

Building a good vocabulary may be even more important in our industry than it is in many others. The general public does not typically think of hair stylists as "professionals." You may not be able to change public opinion about our profession as a whole, but you absolutely can change that perception as it relates to you. When you stand behind your styling chair, draw an imaginary circle around you. That is your area of influence. In that area, you can influence and control everything. The salon and the industry could be falling down around you, but nothing can affect what happens in your circle. You have to use your area of influence to stand out from the crowd to make your own success.

Put a strong vocabulary in your corner. Exercise it by learning a new word each day. With a little progress, you will find it easy to converse with clients across the professional spectrum. This action is a great example of the sort of work you need to engage in to be successful but for which there is no immediate reward. This book will be full of those actions. Do not skip this point or be lazy about its application. This point is as important as all the rest. Remember that you will not reach success by working on just a single skill. You need to build a well-rounded earning machine, and every skill matters. You cannot skip or overlook anything.

The 100 Percent Total Satisfaction Guarantee

Any hairdresser who takes customer service seriously and counts on repeat clientele will offer an unconditional guarantee on all services provided. This guarantee of total satisfaction represents a *no-compromise policy* that places the customer first. You should promise the customer that if she is not satisfied with a service she's received and all of your attempts to satisfy her have failed, you will refund her money—all of it!

The hairdresser committed to quality service is a customer's best guarantee. Unfortunately, at some point you will give a haircut to someone you will not be able to please. When you have given a guest exactly what he or she has asked for and you know you have met your obligation to him or her, it is difficult to accept that you need to offer a refund. However, I assure you that a refund policy is not a liability. You must look at the big picture of things. I committed to offering a 100 percent unconditional guarantee from the day I first established myself as a hairdresser. During my twenty-five-year career, I have had only two clients ask for refunds. Consider that fact: I have given just two refunds in twenty-five years, and I would estimate that I've given over fifty thousand haircuts. Were more than two people dissatisfied with a service I provided over all of those years? Of course! But I was able to make them happy in other ways before a refund became necessary. The fact that I had an unconditional refund policy when all was said and done made people feel confident in me. It let them know that even if I weren't ultimately able to make them happy, in the end I would still consider their feelings first.

What are the components and benefits of a policy that guarantees 100 percent total satisfaction? Firstly and most importantly, you will define yourself as a true business professional by guaranteeing your work. This one simple commitment will establish your reputation with clients. Please believe me on this point: You cannot put a value on your reputation. You need to do everything you can do to bolster your "rep." Besides, all business aside, it's the right thing to do.

When do you advise your client of your guarantee? Always! The more obvious your policy is, the better. Make it as public as possible. Post the guarantee in a visible location in your station. At the end of a new service, remind your guest about your guarantee. Remember that your guarantee doesn't need to revolve around a refund. Your guarantee is about your commitment to doing whatever it takes to make sure your clients are happy. The refund would only be the last resort. When a new service is completed, simply state that if she has any questions or problems regarding her service, she should contact you right away and let you know. Remind her that you will make sure she's happy. The gist of your message is that you stand behind your work and have a 100 percent total satisfaction guarantee for any service you provide. This statement gives the clients confidence in your work, encourages them to purchase your services, and establishes your professional reputation. Make sure your clients know that you are aware that the only way to receive client referrals is to make sure everyone is happy. In other words, this policy is not only right, but it's also good business for you. Honor your guarantee when you need to. I take professional pride is stating that I give every client superior-quality service. I extend this pride to include the two customers cited above who asked for refunds. Both of those dissatisfied customers returned several days after receiving their haircuts. Maybe their friends or significant others didn't like the new look. Who knows? In any event, I attempted to work with the two customers to satisfy their needs. In the end, after evaluating their requests for a range of expensive and time-consuming services and realizing that I could not make them happy, I gladly refunded their money.

Why make a refund? At the beginning of their respective appointments, each of my dissatisfied customers explained to me exactly how she wanted her new cut and style to look. I felt I did exactly what they asked me to do. I asked them before they left if they were happy and if I had given them what they were looking for. In short, I covered all of the bases and did my job. Why, then, did I provide refunds to them when I had given them what they had asked for? I did it for a very simple reason; I wanted to keep my clients happy, and I wanted to keep a strong professional reputation more than I wanted the money that day. We all know the rule of thumb in our business: Do a good haircut, and they'll tell three people. Do a bad haircut, and they'll tell twenty people. My reputation was worth more to me than the money I would've gotten from those two clients. Avoiding negative word of mouth was worth more to me in the long run. All too often we think in the moment. When a hairdresser's rent or car payment is due, she might focus on making as much as she can so she can "get by." But that is thinking in the moment and not looking at the big picture. Don't forget that you are in this for the career—not for the day or the week. When I gave refunds to those clients, they left pleased that I had honored my commitments, and I was pleased that they would have no further impact on my business.

Here is a great example of over-the-top customer service. Nordstrom is a well-known, high-end department store. It is very successful for many reasons, but it is well known for its very liberal "no-questions-asked" return policy. Years ago in California, a great story about Nordstrom and their return policy came out. It went something like this: A man walked into Nordstrom and headed to one of the retail counters. He informed the sales associate that he was there to make a return. The associate assured him that she would be happy to help him. She asked the man what he was returning. The man told the associate that he was returning four tires for his car that he had purchased at this store. The associate was a bit confused and asked a manager for help. After the man let the manager know what he was returning, the manager gently told the man that they don't sell tires at Nordstrom. The man was insistent that he had purchased them there and would not give in; he then challenged the manager to honor their return policy. The manager then asked the man how much he had spent on the tires and quickly gave him a full refund, knowing full well the refund did not need to be made.

After the man left, Nordstrom contacted the local media and issued a press release. The press release recounted the entire refund situation. It also reconfirmed their refund policy as a department store, but at the end of the press release the man wrote, "But please don't bring us your tires." It was genius. For the price of four tires, Nordstrom had simultaneously created a tremendous amount of goodwill and established their reputation as a customer-service-based retail store. You can't buy that kind of advertising. That decision wasn't about money—it was about reputation. If the Nordstrom employees had been thinking in the moment, they would have kicked the man out of the store and missed the golden opportunity to solidify their store's reputation. Write yourself an insurance policy that protects your reputation and builds on it at the same time. Adopt a 100 percent satisfaction guarantee on all of the services you provide, and let your clients know about it!

The Image Game

The world is a marketplace, and one of its most lucrative commodities is physical beauty. Image enhancement is a goal for almost every man, woman, and child. The simple fact is that we care about what others think about us, and that oftentimes what others think about us depends on their perception of us. Perception is king in the hair industry.

Before I begin this chapter, allow me to ask you to keep an open mind. The title I've chosen for this chapter can be an instant "turnoff" for some. Many will say, "That's the one part of the hair industry that I don't like, and I want to stay away from it. I just want to be who I am and not worry about all that fake stuff." I get it. But indulge me for a bit and believe me when I tell you that if you think you can avoid this aspect of our industry, you are being naive. If you place any importance on your personal appearance, how you sound, and the perception people have of you, you play the image game to one degree or another.

My thought on the subject, like many others, is that you need to act deliberately. Don't let anything happen you to by accident. Let's begin. If you think people come into a salon just for a service, then you are overlooking the primary focus of our industry—image enhancement. Beauty appeals to vanity, and a successful hair stylist satisfies a client's basic human desires to look attractive and to be surrounded by attractive people. I know that sounds a bit superficial, but if you give it some thought, you might agree. I want to tell you a couple of true stories that will serve as examples of this idea. When I was in Hair/beauty School, I decided that that if I was going to be in this industry, I was going to be successful. In fact, I decided that if I was going to do hair for a living, I was going to be famous and be a hair stylist to the stars. I lived only twenty minutes from downtown Los Angeles, so I set my sights on Beverly Hills. I had just graduated from beauty school and passed my state board exam. I was ready to work. I went to a very famous and well-known salon on Rodeo Drive and asked for an interview. The manager invited me to come back the next day with my résumé. I had no résumé. Sure, I had competed in several haircutting competitions and had even won a few, but I had nothing to put on a résumé—no experience to speak of.

However, I was so determined to work there that I improvised.

I contacted three of the girls I had gone to beauty school with, I cut and styled their hair as "rock star" as I could, I made them dress in their best nightclub outfits, and I took them back to the salon with me the next day. I walked in with my best hair-stylist swagger and asked to see the manager. When she arrived, I mustered up all of my confidence, said, "Here's my résumé," and pointed to my three dressed-up friends. The manager admitted she had never seen that job application approach before but that she liked my confidence. She sat me down and offered me a job. I was offered an apprenticeship position. I would work in that position for two years. During that time, I would shampoo, apply color, sweep hair, and generally help the stylists. I would receive regular training and advanced education, and by the end of the two years, I would be a rock-star hair stylist. And there was one other thing: For two years, I would receive no pay at all. My working for free was considered my payment for the education I would receive. It would be like I was "paying my dues." I tried to look at the big picture, and I took the job.

My experience there was, in all honesty, really bad. The first day I dived in to work and did everything I could to help. Not only was I treated like everyone's "whipping-boy slave," but I also noticed very early on that nobody was happy—not the stylists, and especially not the clients. Everything that happened seemed to be more of a show than a service. Everyone—the stylists and the clientele—seemed like they were pretending in one-way or another. It was the strangest thing I had ever seen. I went back the next day, determined to adapt and fit in. Midway through the day, I was approached by the salon manager. She pulled me aside and very quietly asked me if I could "manage a foreign accent of some kind." I laughed because I thought she was joking with me. She told me she was serious. It was then that I realized what had struck me as so strange the day before—everyone in the salon had some kind of accent when they spoke. I knew what I needed to do. I very respectfully thanked the manager for the opportunity to work there, and I quit my job. I lasted two days there. I went back to the "real world" with "real people" and built a clientele that allowed me to open my first salon almost exactly one year later.

My very brief sojourn in Beverly Hills is an extreme example, but it makes a good point. The salon manager knew that, in addition to service, her clients demanded a certain mystique and flair that appealed to their vanity and satisfied their desire to be pampered. I learned a great lesson from that first job. I learned that what the salon was really selling was the experience of the salon. What they were selling was an image, and that image— and not the services—was exactly what those clients were buying. Now I'm not suggesting that you model yourself after this example. I'm only suggesting that you recognize the importance that image can have in our business and use that knowledge to benefit you.

I have one more example for you. Back in the seventies and eighties, a very successful hair stylist emerged on the scene. His clientele list included Hollywood movie stars, TV stars, and famous people from many industries. He would tell the story of his humble beginning as follows: He was living in a small apartment. He had no money. He only had a couple of outfits to wear, but they were very nice. He saved every penny he could and bought himself an old used Rolls Royce. Most of the time it didn't run. But when it did, and when he could afford to put gasoline in it, he would put on his best outfit and cruise the streets of Beverly Hills. He would stop and give out his business card to every beautiful person he saw. He would tell them that he was a hairdresser to the stars and that they should let him do their hair. Before long, he actually became what he claimed to be. This man knew how to play the image game. I have a lot of respect for that man. I've always loved his story—not because I wanted to do the same thing, but because I realized the importance of deciding on the image you want to portray and how success-ful you could be if you consciously sell that image.

That is what this chapter is really about. The image game is not about pretending to be something you're not; it's about knowing how important a good image is and making sure you put that image out in everything you do. I built my career in what I call the "real world," which has real working people with regu-lar lives—not Hollywood celebrities. I'm glad I made that choice long ago. Real working people, in my opinion, are a lot more enjoy-able to work with, and, to put it bluntly; their money spends exactly the same.

To parody Shakespeare, a salon is a stage, and every stylist achieving stardom is acting a part. The minute you walk into the salon, you have to remember that for the remainder of the day people will be judging your appearance, grace, style, manner, and skill. I have always told my staff that the moment you walk out onto the floor, you are on stage. People are watching you. You had better make sure that your actions reflect what you are "selling." You have to decide this ahead of time. Again, I'm not suggesting you sell yourself as something you're not. On the contrary, I think it's much easier to maintain a consistent image if you aren't fake. Be yourself, but be conscious of the fact that you will sell an image of yourself whether it's deliberate or not. The only question is what that image will be. To help you win the image game, I offer the following tips for success:

> **Dressing right.** The way you dress is the ultimate tool when it comes to image. It does not depend on the money you spend on your clothing. It depends more on how you put those clothes together and how the clothes look. Looking manicured and professional is what really matters. Clients need to see that you take time getting ready for work. Simply making sure your clothes are pressed makes a huge difference in how you are perceived by people. You do not need

to "dress up," but you should always look neat and clean, and you should always look better than your clients. Clothing is expensive, and putting a nice wardrobe together isn't easy when you're just starting out. So let's just say you have three nice outfits that you could wear into the salon. You put those outfits together well every day, and you alternate your outfits every day. The other stylists may know that you only wear three different outfits, but your clients only come in every five to six weeks. It will take them a while to figure that out, and by the time they do, you will have built your wardrobe. Don't worry about that. Look good and build your wardrobe as you go.

Showing off. Attend trade shows and watch hairdressers do their work on stage. Watch their body posture, their movements, and their positioning. Observe how they are "working it." I'm not suggesting that you act phony—that is not the lesson I want to teach. However, do remember to show class and style, to charm them with your wit, and above all to let them know that you love your job. Have a good time while you work—even when you don't feel like it. Stage actors call this "method acting." There is nothing wrong with it in our industry. Remember that you can't afford to look like you're having a bad day. You have to present an image of yourself that is consistent. I have always felt very strongly about this point. I told my staff that if they couldn't come in to the salon and be "on," it would be better to not come to work that day at all. You can't afford to come into the salon and present an image of yourself that will contradict the one you've been working so hard to sell.

Appreciating your own work. Do not overlook this small tip. Once or twice during a cut on a client, physically step back one or two feet and look at your work. It is a great way to check for balance, shape, and symmetry; it also draws attention from your client and others in the salon. Work it! This tactic sends a clear message to the person in your chair and to clients throughout the salon that you are conscientious about your work. It also says that you're not afraid to appreciate your own work. Remember that people don't like arrogance but they love confidence. Do this, and you can be certain that your "show" will attract future clients to your chair. Remember that you're on stage, and act like it. Do not make the mistake of staring at the back of your client's head throughout the service. Don't be like all of the other hairdressers who do this. Move around and be seen.

Avoiding the mirror mistake. Do not—do not—ever turn your guest away from the mirror. This is one of the clearest signs of low self-confidence that a hairdresser can show. Is that the image you want to sell? How can your guest see how to style her hair if she's facing the wall? How can your guest see you appreciate your work? How can your guest see you enjoy your job? How can you have eye contact with your guest when you talk? I could go on and on. Don't do it! If you need to turn your guest away from the mirror because your blow dryer cord is too short, buy a new blow dryer! Don't do it! This single act says, "I'm scared" more than any other. If you're not going to show confidence, you might as well go home.

Don't be fake or phony, but be conscious of how you look, sound, and act at all times.

Realize that an image of you is being sold at all times, whether you like it or not. If there are sides of your personality that don't fit the image you want to sell, maybe it's best not to bring those personality traits out on stage with you. Maybe it's best they stay in the break room or even at home. I will say this in many ways throughout this book: this industry requires conscious effort. It's not difficult, but you must be deliberate in your decisions and in your actions.

Station Location

Location, location, location! Yes, I know it's the mantra of realtors across America. It also happens to be one of the more crucial decisions you can make when it comes to picking "your spot" in a salon.

There apparently exist two very different points of view on station location. Some hairdressers prefer a more private corner to work and service clientele in. They feel that they are providing a more private and quiet environment for their guests. Other stylists want to be out in the open where the crowd can see their work. We'll examine both lines of thinking.

Hairdressers who favor privacy do so because they believe it makes the client feel more at ease. One presumption is that female clients do not want to be seen while having their services done. In my opinion, this perspective is a bit sexist, but many hairdressers stand by this principle. A few hairdressers go so far as to maintain a private room for their appointments. They also feel they can be more personable with clients and that the privacy is a plus when it comes to building a clientele.

As you may have already guessed, I have a different view. I regard privacy as isolation and isolation as the successful hairdresser's enemy. While the privacy perspective isn't necessarily wrong, it does limit your clientele. Most people like to be around other people. And while they may appreciate all the work you put in to your beautiful little room, most people will want to be where the fun is and want to have a larger experience. Besides, we have already spoken about the importance of acting like you're on stage at all times. A stage for one isn't very motivating for an ambitious stylist. Some clients like privacy, but most like the "show." Your best chance of success is to make most of the people happy at all times. Go with what the larger number of people want, and realize that your best chance of success is to be seen. In this matter, put your business concerns ahead of your clients. The more your work is seen, the greater interest it will generate.

Some clients will not feel the same as you do on this subject. They will actually leave you to sit in a quieter spot with another stylist. Your first thought might be, "I can't lose any clients. I have to make everyone happy." Get over it! You'll never make everyone happy. You are in this for the big picture. You must make your decisions based on what will make your career advance on a large scale and not client-by-client. That client who left you would've eventually gone to a more "low-key" stylist anyway. It's inevitable. Not every personality will match with yours. As you build your clientele, you will find that certain personalities will be drawn to you and others will move away from you. It's OK; it is the way of things. After building your clientele for some time, you will realize that somehow, most of your clients are "magically" a lot like you. That makes it easy to be yourself and to continue to enjoy your work; that makes your clients happy.

Public exposure (not that kind, silly) promotes professionalism. In a highly visible location, you are more likely to push for excellence in every category. You're more likely to cover all of the bases when you know others are watching. You're more likely to be motivated to be "on stage," and you will definitely attract more new clients by being out in the open and visible. Make your decisions based on what's best for business, not based on your emotions.

Prebooking

Prebooking appointments is the single most important business practice for building and maintaining a large and lucrative clientele base. The following paragraphs outline the prebooking process and discuss how pre-booking works to your benefit.

Prebooking establishes a routine appointment schedule for clients. This very basic point is critical for both you and your clients. To really get this point, let's first look at how the vast majority of people handle their hair appointments. Most people start thinking about their hair when it's either hard to style or when it doesn't look right any longer. In other words, they start thinking about setting an appointment after their hair is already out of shape.

When your client calls the salon to make an appointment and finds out that the first available appointment you have is two weeks away, the situation becomes worse in many ways. It now becomes your job to "fit her in" to your busy schedule—that is, if you want to make sure she doesn't go somewhere else. Meanwhile, your schedule has been disrupted to accommodate her. For your clients, the main benefit of setting up a scheduling routine is making sure they are back in your chair before their hair starts to look bad. If their hair never has the chance to get out of shape, they will get more compliments, and more compliments will make them more likely to refer people to you. For the client, a prebooking schedule simply means that they are less likely to go through a time when their hair doesn't look good or is hard to manage. That's a good thing for them, and incidentally it makes you look pretty good, too. The benefit to you as a hairdresser and as a businessperson is huge.

Prebooking permits you to maintain a smaller client base. Let's look at two different hair stylists. One stylist does not prebook her clients, and the other does. Let's say that both stylists have a client base of one hundred fifty people that they see on a regular basis. For the sake of easy math and simple numbers, let's just say that each of the stylists only provides haircuts for their clientele— neither of them provides chemical services, and both stylists charge exactly the same amount for their haircuts. We will call our stylist who does not prebook her appointments Alexa. Alexa doesn't try to encourage her guests to schedule their next appointments before they leave the salon. She feels the practice is too pushy and thinks that her clients appreciate her easygoing attitude. Besides, she tried it a couple of times, and it made her feel very uncomfortable. Alexas' clients are on their own and schedule and come in when they feel they need to be seen. On average, she will see each client about every eight weeks for a haircut. Alexa charges forty dollars for a haircut and style.

OK—if Alexa gives a haircut and style to each of her 150 clients every 8 weeks, she will see each of them 6 times every year. She will have about 19 appointments every week—that's almost 4 appointments every day if she works 5 days a week. She will earn $40 for each haircut and style she gives. At that rate, Alexa will earn $800 every week. For Alexa, that means $3,200 in monthly income and a yearly income of $38,400. This is gross income for Alexa, meaning that this is her income before any work-related expenses she may have.

Now let's look at our stylist who does pre-book her clients' appointments before they leave the salon. We will call her Nikki. Because Nikki prebooks her clients, she will see each of them about every 6 weeks. If her clients come in about every 6 weeks, Nikki will see each of them about 8 or 9 times each year. With her clients coming in every 6 weeks, she will have about 25 appointments on her appointment book every week—that's about 5 appointments every day if Nikki works 5 days each week. Nikki will earn $40 for each haircut and style she gives. At that rate, Nikki will earn $1,000 every week. That would translate to a monthly income of $4,000 and a yearly income of $48,000.

I know the discrepancy in Alexa and Nikki's incomes is significant, but that's not the real point here. If Alexa does not keep her clientele of 150 people on a regular booking schedule by pre-booking their appointments before they leave the salon, she will need to build her clientele to 222 people just to make the same yearly income as Nikki. Let me say that another way: Alexa has to build and maintain a clientele of 222 people just to make the same yearly income as Nikki, who has only 150 clients. Both of the ladies are doing the exact same work and charging the exact same prices. The only difference is that one of them is prebooking her appointments, and the other is not.

If we use the same two ladies as an example and factor chemical services into their incomes, the difference between the two becomes a bit more significant. Let's say that the average chemical service is about $60, and let's say for argument's sake that 50 percent of each of the two stylists' clients receive a chemical service on a regular basis. Here is the bottom line: Alexa would make an average of $65,000 a year. Nikki would make an average of $86,000 a year.

The contrast becomes even more apparent when we factor in the extra income each of the stylists would earn if she double-booked her appointments. That is what results in a true six-figure income. I will cover that in the next chapter.

In the example, Alexa has essentially lost $21,000 each and every year just because she decided not to prebook her clients. Now in the world I live in, $21,000 a year is a pretty decent amount of money when it comes to a standard of living. It's an especially large amount of money when you consider that all Alexa would've needed to do was change the way she works and make it an important business rule. This is just a decision—nothing more.

The psychology of prebooking. Yes, there is a psychological advantage to prebooking your appointments, and that advantage will benefit both your income and your reputation. How does it work? Believe it or not, all you have to do is prebook your appointments and it will work for you.

Let me explain. I'll give one simple example of how this works. Susie is a client of yours. You prebook all of her appointments five to six weeks in advance before she leaves the salon (as you should every time). Susie has an appointment set up with you in about a week or so. She gets a call from her friend Kate, who wants to get together next Saturday. Well, Kate wants to get together at the exact time that Susie has an appointment with you. So Susie tells Kate she can't meet at that time because she has a hair appointment then.

Kate says something like "just reschedule your appointment." Susie tells Kate that she can't just reschedule. She lets Kate know that she has to set up her appointments with you about six weeks in advance and that if she tries to reschedule it, there's no telling how long it will take her to get back in with you.

Even if it's not a conscious thought, Kate will wonder why you are in such demand. She may even wonder what makes you so special that Susie needs to book an appointment five to six weeks in advance. She may decide that she needs to find out for herself and needs to ask Susie for your phone number. Get the idea?

When something is scarce, it's in demand. In this case, that something is you. It's not enough to know how this concept works; you have to use it, too. You have to make it happen. We will talk about that next.

Keep in mind that this same psychology also works on your regular clients—not just on the new ones. They won't necessarily know why you prebook them before they leave; they'll just know that you do it. It's how you do business. Most of your guests will assume that you prebook because your schedule is busy. Let them think that even if it's not exactly the truth just yet.

Let me give you a personal example of how this has worked for me. I was fresh out of hair school and working my first job in a salon. (This was just after my Beverly Hills salon job that "didn't work out.") Let me first say that I did not come up with this by myself. I wish I were that cool and smart. I had the advantage of an amazing mentor who taught me everything, and this was a purely Johnny Hernandez technique.

I had no clientele. When you first start out, you start with zero. That meant that every person who walked into the salon and sat in my chair was a first-time client for me. When Johnny first told me about this idea, he asked me a simple rhetorical question: "When do you pre-book clients? Is it after they come in for their second appointment with you? Do you start the process then?" The answer was obvious: "It's the first time and every time after."

So the situation was as follows: I had a clientele base of zero, and I was expected to prebook every new person who sat down in my chair. How was I to do that? Why would I have needed to do that? If I had been really busy and in demand, prebooking would have been necessary. But I was not any of those things. "Not yet you aren't," he said. "But you will be if you act like it."

He taught me a simple concept that he called "fake it till you make it." The idea is that perception is everything. Remember the example in the chapter "The Image Game" of the famous hair stylist who drove the Rolls Royce? The perception of his success was what made him successful at first. He created an image and a perception of himself that he sold. You will do the same.

You will not be fake or false, but you will deliberately create the perception that you are busy now and that you have a large clientele now. People will respond positively, and you will build your clientele twice as fast—period. That is what I did.

When I first started out in the business, very few salons were computerized, and everyone used a handwritten "week-at-a-glance" appointment book. When I finished a hair service, I would walk my guest up to the front desk and start the prebooking process. When I got up to the desk, my main goal was to make sure my clients never saw my appointment book. I didn't want them to see it because it was empty. So I made sure I kept it under the top of the desk when I went through the prebooking. (A year later, I loved pulling out my appointment book so it could be seen, but at that time I did not.)

Whenever I prebooked a guest, I used a simple trick Johnny called "the fifteen-minute rule." It was simple and helped me accomplish everything I wanted to. I went through my prebook script (which I'll discuss later) and came to the point where I would ask, "What time would work for you?" When my client told me his or her answer, my little show would begin.

I would pause to look at my appointment book (which was empty and hidden under the top of the desk) and after considerable thought, I would say, "How about one forty-five or two fifteen?" No matter what time the client asked for, I would suggest scheduling an appointment for fifteen minutes before or after it. That gave them the idea that I was busy and was trying to fit them in. I didn't need to tell a lie or be ridiculous in some way, and it made me seem like I was in demand even on my first day. If a client really had to have that two o'clock time slot, I would pause and say, "It'll be fine. I can make that work."

The point wasn't to force my will on my guests and make them take the time slot I chose. The point was to prebook their next appointments before they left. That way, I could leave them with the impression that I was busy and in demand, and then I could capitalize on that perception. Fake it till you make it, folks. There's nothing wrong with a bit of theater. People buy perception, so you might as well create some. Besides, if you're consistent, you won't have to fake it for long.

Prebooking is not just for you. Prebooking has some very real benefits for clients. For one thing, it serves as a guarantee that you will be available when they need you and at a time that is convenient for them. Time is a very valuable commodity for most people.

Prebooking also serves as your commitment to provide a service to them. It's a commitment that you will be available to them in five to six weeks to refresh a cut, brighten a color, or simply make sure they still look their best. Keeping your guests on a regular schedule allows you to make sure that their hair never develops a problem or becomes difficult for them to handle. That is good for everyone, and your clients will appreciate it.

This brings up a good point. Let's say that your client is new to you but has never been to a stylist who prebooked her appointments before she left the salon. Let's just say that her last stylist never made prebooking a priority and simply waited for her to call in when she needed a service. Your new client is used to getting in about every seven to eight weeks; she has certainly been through times when her hair was really giving her trouble and she couldn't wait until her next appointment.

Let's just say that her last stylist and you are about the same technically and do the same quality of work. However, she is now prebooking all of her appointments ahead of time and coming in about every five to six weeks, which will prevent her hair from getting out of hand. The only thing your client knows is that now that she is with you, she never goes through a period of time when she has trouble with her hair; her hair always looks good. She may never make the connection, but the main reason that she always looks good is because she prebooks—it's not necessarily because of her stylist. If that is the case, there is nothing wrong with accepting responsibility for her happiness. But realize that prebooking or not prebooking can change the whole picture.

Your client is a walking billboard for you and for herself. This will either work for you or against you, but it works whether you like it or not. If your clientele base always prebooks and always comes in to see you about every five to six weeks, you will have a clientele base that looks good. Again, this is good for all of you. When you have clients walking around whose hair never has the chance to get out of shape, your walking billboards will bring you business. But when you have clients walking around who don't have a booking schedule and don't always look their best, your billboards will work against you and will hurt your business. It's just that simple. Prebooking is not an option. You must do it, or you will struggle in this industry.

How to prebook: You must work to make this a part of how you do business. Prebooking needs to be done for every client—no exceptions. With that said, I should note that prebooking will become routine once you develop the skill and confidence necessary to use it consistently as you build and maintain your business. The process intimidates many hairdressers, and many think it is confrontational and too assertive. I am going to help you work through these anxieties by demonstrating two different prebooking scenarios.

The first scenario involves prebooking a new client, and the second involves prebooking an existing client for the first time. These scenarios were developed to be scripts. Rehearse them with a coworker, a family member, or a friend until you feel comfortable with the routine. Now when I say rehearse them, I really mean it. It must appear to your clientele that prebooking is second nature to you. It must seem as natural as walking. If your efforts to prebook come off as contrived or scripted (even though they are scripted), your guests will feel it. If your clients feel it, so will you, and you will be less likely to continue.

Note that the more you prebook your guests, the more comfortable and effective you will be. But do not read this and just start practicing it on your clientele. There is homework involved. Rehearse it many times before you do it with your clients—especially your existing clients. Nothing will discourage you more than an existing client who gives you the feeling that she thinks you're trying to "sell" her on something or not acting like yourself. I have seen many stylists start this process unprepared. They are the first ones to give up after one or two negative experiences. To get the best results, you need to already be good at prebooking before you prebook your first client. Don't go into this unprepared. Don't be that stylist.

Ask your friends and family to sometimes respond as a client who doesn't like to prebook. Tell them to make it hard on you. This will help you handle any prebooking situation and will make sure you won't get flustered when someone gives you resistance. So rehearse your prebooking scripts until you are sick of them, and then do it more. I promise it will pay off.

New client. You just finished a service on a new client; this was her first time seeing you as a stylist. Let's just say you gave her a haircut and style. You describe the retail products that you used, tell her what you recommend, put them on the desk, and say, "Let the receptionist know what you want to do with those." Then you simply ask, "How many weeks do you usually go between haircuts?" It is very likely that she will ask what you recommend. You tell her that almost all of your clients are in about every five to six weeks. (That means five weeks, by the way!)

Then you say, "Let's see where that puts us," as you look at your calendar. This is a critical point in the prebooking process. It is very important that you don't look up or pause at all. You simply look on the calendar to see where five weeks from the day lands, and then you say, "Is this time of day good for you?" She will respond and let you know what time of day to look for, or she will show some reluctance about prebooking her appointment ahead of time. (If she is reluctant, refer to your script.) Now book the appointment and give her a card with the date and time on it. Done.

If she is reluctant to prebook, tell her something like, "Calling for your next appointment is fine. I just try to encourage my clients to book ahead because by doing that we make sure you get the time you need. If there's a problem on your end, you can always call to reschedule, but at least you'll be on the books." The message they should receive from you is that this process and practice is for them, not you. This is an extension of the service you provide them in the chair. You're doing her a favor by suggesting this.

If your guest is still reluctant to prebook, then you're done. Do not push it! It's not a favor if it's shoved down her throat. Simply say one last thing: "No problem at all. Try to call ahead as much as you can, but if there's nothing available when you call in, ask the receptionist to get me to the phone and I'll see if I can find a time slot."

Again, you are emphasizing that this process is for her, not you. You have also planted the seed of the idea that she may not get an appointment with you when she calls. That is a good thing. Even if you're still in the fake-it-till-you-make-it phase, the reality is that very soon you will be too busy to allow your clients to just call in when they want. Prebooking will be a necessity, and without it you will end up saying no to people when they try to book appointments on their own. If this happens a lot to a client, she will find someone else. Getting your clients used to prebooking their appointments will also help you to retain them for longer periods of time.

Personal note: After three years in the business, I had a 98 percent prebooking rate with my clientele, and over 60 percent of those clients prebooked two appointments ahead. (Almost all of my chemical-service clients booked two appointments ahead.) I didn't hit those numbers because I was cooler than my coworkers; I hit those numbers because I was consistent with my prebooking practice. After only three years, I was so busy that my clients *had* to prebook with me just to get on my schedule. That is a good position for a hairdresser to be in, yes?

By the way, don't you want to know what your income will be five weeks from now? Do you want to just wonder and hope? Do you want to say, "Gee, I hope all of my clients call in for appointments soon, because I really need to make my car payment"? Really? Think about that.

Existing client. It's always harder to bring existing clients around to new ideas. Your current clients know you—they know how you operate, and they have a point of reference with you. I know it can be a bit unnerving to change things up with your existing clients, but you have to do it anyway! Get over it.

I had a simple attitude with my existing clients regarding prebooking: it was for their benefit. When any client would ask why she needed to start prebooking, I would simply say something like, "With all the new clients coming in to me now, I want to make sure that those of you who have taken care of me all of this time always get the time you need. I don't want the new people to edge you out."

This whole concept is about your core attitude and confidence. If you truly believe that prebooking isn't beneficial for your guests, it won't work. If you can't muster up enough confidence to believe in the process, people will sense it and tell you no. This, like many of the ideas in this book, depends on your frame of mind. One encouraging point to consider is that you can control your frame of mind. You are in charge.

So you have just finished a service on a guest you have been seeing awhile now. You walk her to the front as you always do. This time, you must initiate a new subject with her. I will not try to script it for you. This really needs to come from your personality, or it will seem contrived. But I will suggest something that has worked for me. I do it as if it has just crossed my mind or as if I have just thought of it.

"Oh hey, Marie, lately I have been having a lot of trouble getting my regular clients on my schedule. I want to make sure that all of the new people coming to me now don't edge you guys out. So I'm making sure I set up all of my regulars ahead of time from now on. If the date becomes a problem, you can always reschedule." Note that I am not asking. I'm not forcing, but I'm not asking. I am letting her know that this is what I need to do from now on to take care of her. This is how business is being conducted, and it's for her benefit! Again, it's all about frame of mind and confidence.

As I look at my calendar, I say, "I know we usually go about five weeks between haircuts. Let's see where that puts us." Now that I am at this point, I prebook my existing client just the same as I would a new client. The only difference would be if she were reluctant to prebook. In that case, I would have the same posture, but I would obviously handle it differently depending on my relationship with her. Make no mistake, though—she is getting prebooked eventually.

In a perfect world, I would prebook each and every client with no problems at all. They would all love the idea and would know that I simply had their best interests in mind. Well, it's not a perfect world. Surprised? Good, I hoped not. Then you won't mind getting over your fears on the subject and just getting down to business. I've said this already, but it bears repeating: This is a no-option subject. You must do this. If prebooking doesn't come as naturally to you as it does to others, try harder. If you just can't seem to handle it when someone gives you resistance, rehearse more. Don't give up.

Know that some people will jump right on board and prebook the first time you bring it up. Some people will need to come visit you for five appointments in a row and hear you go through your script five times before they finally start to pre-book. Some people will need to actually be told, "No, I can't get you in right now," before they get the message. And some people will never prebook with you at all. It doesn't matter. What is important is that you are consistent with each and every person who sits in your chair. Do not judge who will and who will not pre-book. Everyone is handled the same.

Prebooking is one of those skills that we work to become proficient at but that doesn't yield immediate results. Prebooking is a big-picture skill. Know that ahead of time, and don't expect to see growth the next week after you start. Trust in the process, keep your mind right, and keep your confidence high.

To succeed in this business, you need a styling chair, shears, a blow dryer, and prebooking. Get it? Enough said?

On the following page I have provided a simple prebooking script to use as a guideline.

Prebooking Script

DO NOT ASK If THEY WANT TO PRE-BOOK AN APPOINTMENT

Scenario 1:

"How long do you usually go between hair-cuts? What's normal"?

Wait for an answer.

"Great, let's see where that puts us."

Go right to the calendar and find a date. Do not look up—just do it.

"That puts us about [date]. Is this a good day of the week for you? Does this time of day work too?"

Book the appointment and write the date and time on a card for her. Done.

Scenario 2: If the client says, "I usually just call in for my appointments."

"That's fine, but you may just want to put your-self on the books to make sure you have a time set. If there's a conflict, you can always move it, but at least you'll have an appointment on the books." (Create a sense of urgency.)

Wait for an answer.

Scenario 3: If the client says, "I'll just call in."

"No problem—just try to give me as much notice as possible. If you have a problem get-ting in, just ask the receptionist to get me to the phone, and I'll do what I can to fit you in."

Tracking Your Business

Tracking your business goes hand in hand with prebooking. Most salons will operate on a computer system that will make tracking easier, and many of the numbers the salon owners' watch will be available to you. If the salon you work at does not have a computer, you still need to track your numbers. I will show you how to calculate your numbers manually just in case you don't have those numbers available to you on a computer. Make no mistake, though: Tracking your numbers and your business is not an option. It is a "must-do" item and has to be done without fail if you want to succeed. As I have said repeatedly, you need to operate like a businessperson and not like someone who has a hobby. If you do not track your numbers, you will never know if you are making progress. You will never know if your efforts are paying off. I use the phrase "don't let this business happen to you" with my staff quite a lot. Be aware of what's happening, and stay in control of it. Tracking is one of the best ways to do that, and it also has a unique way of keeping us motivated and confident. You can't know where you're going if you don't first know where you've been.

Every week you will track specific information for a specific purpose. Here is your list:

> Total number of guests, number of requests, number of referrals, number of prebooks, prebook percentage, number of add-on services, number of chemical services, chemical to service percentage, retail to service percentage, retail sales percentage, service totals, retail totals, and average ticket/ client dollar amount.

I have put all of these tracking items on an easy-to-follow chart (the "Weekly Stylist Analysis" form on the next page) and will explain each of them in detail. I will also show you how to track each item without the help of a computer just in case your salon doesn't track these items.

Weekly Stylist Analysis

Name _____   Week Ending _____

Total Number of Guests _____

Number of Requests _____

Number of Referrals _____

How Many Pre-booked? _____   Prebook Percentage _____

Total Add-On Services _____

(Condition/shine treatments, brow makeover, added chemical services, etc.)

Total Number of Services _____

Total Number of Chemicals _____   Chemical to Service Percentage _____

Total Retail $ _____

Total Service $ _____   Retail to Service Percentage _____

Service & Retail Total $ _____   Average Ticket/ Client $_____

Next Week Goals

Guests _____

Referrals _____

Pre-booked _____

Add-On Services _____

New Chemicals _____

Retail Sales _____

Tracking your numbers is critical to building your business. If you consistently track your business, you will find it much, much easier to grow your business. It's just that simple. Here is how you will do it without the use of a computer.

When you track your numbers, you need to look at three different "snapshots"—daily, weekly, and monthly. I have provided a weekly sheet in this book. You can simply make copies of that page and write in daily, weekly, or monthly depending on the numbers you happen to be tracking. But understand that tracking is something you do every day. I started out with five daily tracking sheets that I would add up and transfer to a weekly tracking sheet, which I would then add up and transfer to a monthly tracking sheet at the end of the month. That's a simple concept, but some people have trouble calculating the numbers, so let's do that next.

Tracking the number of guests you see in a week and the number of guests who prebook their appointments in a week is easy. But what about figuring out a prebook percentage? In other words, what if you wanted to know the percentage of clients who prebooked that week? (And you do want to know that number because it's a percentage that you want to grow every week.)

Here is what you do. Let's say you saw 30 guests the entire week. Out of those 30 guests, 12 of them prebooked their next appointments before they left the salon. To get the percentage, you would divide the large number into the small number and press the percentage button (%) on your calculator. (So divide 12 by 30 and then press the percentage button. That equals 40.) In this case, you would have a 40 percent prebooking rate for that week. We will use this same formula to get all of our other percentages.

What about finding out what your chemical to service percentage is? In other words, out of all the services you did, what percentage were chemical services? Let's say that during the same week you actually provided 40 total services. Of the 40 services, 10 of them were chemical services. To figure out the chemical to service percentage, you will divide the large number into the small number and hit the percentage button on your calculator. Don't hit the equal button. It will not work. (Divide 10 by 40 and then press the percentage button. That equals 25.) In this example, you have a 25 percent chemical to service percentage. Are you starting to get the idea?

Stop and pick up a calculator while you're reading this. Try the formula a few times—it will make this seem a lot less foreign.

Now let's figure out your retail to service percentage. Think of it like this: out of all the service dollars you generated, what percentage of that number was from retail sales?

Let's say that you generated $1,000 in service for the entire week. During that week, you also recommended $150 in retail products. To calculate the service to retail percentage, you would divide the large number into the small number and press the percentage key on your calculator. (Divide 150 by 1,000 and then press the percentage button. That equals 15.) So in this case you would have a 15 percent retail to service percentage.

Now let's figure out what your average ticket/client dollar amount is. In other words, on average, how much are your clients spending when they sit down in your chair? First add up your service and retail total amounts. If we use the example above, that number would be $1,150 of total services and retail. In the example above, you saw a total of 30 guests for the week. In this case, we will divide the small number into the large number because we are not trying to calculate a percentage—we are just calculating a dollar amount number. (Divide 1,150 by 30. That equals 38.33.) So in this case, each client who sat down in your chair spent an average of $38.33. Get it?

After a while, these numbers start sounding like—well, just like a bunch of numbers. The reason you need to track and know what these numbers are is because it's the best and easiest way to know if your efforts are paying off. It's the best way to know if you are moving in the right direction or if you need to change what you are doing.

Much of what we do in this business is subjective and based on personality and emotion. Tracking your business can't be! Tracking your business needs to be cold, and it needs to be "black and white." This happens behind the scenes and is never something that any guest would or should know is even happening. This is business maintenance, and if you don't do it, I guarantee you that you will not know where you are going. You will "let this business happen to you."

The second part of our Weekly Stylist Analysis Sheet is the goals section. This is pretty straightforward. Look at your numbers from the last week and set some reasonable and attainable goals for the next week. Track your progress to see if what you're doing is working.

Looking at the actual numbers is good, but sometimes there can be a pretty big difference between one new chemical service a day and what you were doing before. That is why I spent the time to help you figure out your percentage numbers.

Watch your percentage numbers. The point of tracking is to know what direction your business is heading in. Percentage numbers will give you a more detailed look at your progress. After you have built a decent-sized clientele, it's harder to see if you've made a large jump forward just by looking at the base numbers.

Looking at your percentage numbers will show you the very small increases and decreases, allow you to make appropriate changes, and keep you motivated. As you build your clientele, your weekly goals will become percentage goals, and your tracking will always retain its meaning and importance.

Double Booking

The income you make as a hair stylist is limited by two factors: your own effort—that is, the hustle you put forth to generate and maintain client—and time, which controls the amount of work you can physically do during each workday. This manual has discussed practices that will allow you to increase your earning potential as a hairdresser. The second factor, time, is beyond our control. There are, after all, only twenty-four hours during each day. Nonetheless, you can make time work for you in a way that increases the number of clients you can schedule on a daily basis. How? By using a scheduling process called "double-booking." Double-booking appointments maximizes time and increases your hourly income.

The successful hairdresser will use double booking to schedule appointments between chemicals or any other service that involves downtime. Many hairdressers take the position that double booking violates professional ethics or makes a hairdresser look greedy. If you feel that way, get over it. Like with everything else in our industry, there is a right way and a wrong way to do it. If done correctly, double booking is a legitimate business practice and an efficient tool for building your business.

On the surface, double booking appears to contradict our professional creed to give superior service to one client at a time. On the other hand, double booking can be a vital tool in the professional hairdresser's arsenal, and it can expand his or her clientele base. This apparent contradiction is the industry's Catch-22. Fortunately, we can solve this tricky problem with some simple time management and (maybe) a little help.

There is no question that professional hairdressers want to treat each guest as if she is the only client of the day. This level of service is how we build a thriving business and an excellent reputation. However, you also need to consider the larger economic picture. To achieve a happy medium, it is necessary for you to balance your artistic and professional self; you need to remember the logical side of operating a successful business. I suggest that double- booking allows you to satisfy both goals. In fact, I know it does.

To double-book effectively, you need to know how much time is required to perform each service you offer and how to schedule appointments without conflict. Not only do you need to know your service times, but you also have to be consistent with your service times and always try your best not to run late on each service. As we move forward, you will see that if you're not consistent with your service times, a five-minute delay on each service throughout the day could mean a forty-five- to sixty-minute delay for your last guest of the evening.

First develop a list of services you offer. Then estimate the time it takes to perform each service and mark this time next to the appropriate service on your list. It would also be helpful to include your prices for each service on this list. Your receptionist should have a copy of this list to ensure that your appointments will be scheduled correctly. Keep a copy of this list at your workstation also. I have provided a sample list on the following page that can be used as a guide.

Successful double booking depends on your ability to schedule and service two appointments during an overlapping time frame without creating conflict— and without losing your cool. I offer the following example to help you understand how this can work.

Illustration one: In this example, our client Sue Jones has an appointment with you for a perm and haircut at three in the afternoon. Your service schedule shows that a perm and haircut would require a two-hour appointment. Without double booking, the normal routine would be to block out two hours for the appointment (from three to five). By looking at your schedule of services, it is clear that the first forty-five minutes of the appointment with Sue will involve wrapping the perm, applying the chemical, and waiting for the perm to take hold for thirty minutes. Sue's appointment will then be finished with a haircut that will take approximately forty-five minutes. It is during the chemical processing time that you can fit in an appointment for a second haircut.

This is the point where you need to be careful with your double-booking decisions. In your appointment schedule, you have Sue Jones booked for a perm and a haircut at three in the afternoon; place an X at the three-forty-five time slot to indicate availability for your next appointment. Don't forget to indicate how much total time is needed for the entire appointment on your schedule. Make sure it is very clear and simple to see. If you aren't clear, you will make mistakes, and you will make it very difficult for your receptionist to schedule you properly. Mistakes mean someone usually gets upset. That someone is usually your client. And it's very hard to keep our cool when our client is upset.

Pam Smith calls your salon for a haircut appointment. She accepts the three-forty-five time slot that follows the chemical treatment for Sue Jones. Your appointment schedule now shows that you have two clients scheduled during the same appointment period—this is double booking. How do you handle both appointments? The answer is easier than you think.

Service Times and Prices

Staff Member _____

Work Schedule

Sun. _____ Mon. _____ Tues. _____ Wed. _____ Thurs. _____ Fri. _____ Sat. _____

Time needed _____ Price_____

Haircut Woman   _____   _____

Haircut Man   _____   _____

Haircut Child   _____   _____

Combination Services

Permanent Color & Cut   _____   _____

Full Foil & Cut   _____   _____

Partial Foil & Cut   _____   _____

Permanent Color/ Foil/ Cut   _____   _____

Permanent Wave & Cut   _____   _____

Relaxer/Straight & Cut   _____   _____

Single Services without Cut

Permanent Color   _____   _____

Semi perm Color   _____   _____

Foil short/med hair   _____   _____

Foil long hair   _____   _____

Perm short/med hair   _____   _____

Perm long hair   _____   _____

Spiral perm   _____   _____

Relaxer/Straight   _____   _____

Formal/Up-do Style   _____   _____

Shampoo & Style   _____   _____

This sheet should be at the front desk so appointments can be made correctly.

Sue Jones arrives at three for her perm. You will shampoo her, wrap her, and apply her perm by three forty-five. Find a comfortable spot for Sue to sit while her perm processes. Pam Smith comes in at three forty-five for her haircut. As you prepare to work on Pam, tell her that during her cut you will need to stop for a few minutes to rinse off a chemical that is processing on another guest.

In my experience, as long as people know what they can expect, they are usually OK. It's when something is a surprise that people tend to get annoyed. Just let your client know what's happening ahead of time. Don't make an apology—you're not sorry that you're busy. Just let him or her know.

Now back to the two clients in your chairs. Fifteen to twenty minutes into your appointment with Pam Smith, you will need to rinse the first solution from Sue Jones's hair. Following the rinse, apply the neutralizer and return to work on Pam. In approximately five minutes, you will need to rinse the neutralizer from Sue's hair. After rinsing the neutralizer, allow Sue to sit—offer her a fresh cup of coffee or another drink—and return to finish Pam. Pam's cut should be finished between four twenty and four thirty. You now have thirty to forty minutes to cut and style Sue before your five o'clock appointment arrives. Easy.

Sound crazy? It's not. Like most things discussed in this book, it all depends on your attitude and your frame of mind. The good news is that you can con-trol both of those by simply making a choice to view the situation in a certain way.

Most clients understand and realize that there is only one of you and that you're in demand. As long as they know ahead of time what the situation is, and as long as you don't take them for granted, they will be fine. People want to see you busy. Isn't that the image you want to sell anyway? Be confident.

Double booking requires a certain com-mitment, but the monetary rewards that come from a heavy client schedule are worth it. Still, double booking is not as hectic as it may seem. Trust me when I say that you will still have time to pay attention to detail and to be personable with your clients.

The secret to staying consistent with your service times is your attitude. Don't ever apologize for being busy. This isn't a hobby; this is your business and your livelihood.

When you decide to practice double booking, it is important that you develop a scheduling process that works for you. If you are concerned about crowding your appointments too close together, add some extra time in between scheduled appointments. You can control this completely. You can always tighten things up later after you have become comfortable. If you are having trouble handling double-bookings, recruit an assistant to help you. An assistant will shampoo, rinse out chemicals, and apply conditioners and neutralizers without significant supervision. This will give you extra time to work on chemical treatments and haircuts within your crowded schedule. We will talk more about the use of an assistant later in the chapter called "The Assistant Advantage."

In the example above, I completed both guests' treatment in a two-hour time period. Although that is very realistic, you can certainly allow additional time in between appointments. For example, if you know you will double-book in between every perm and cut appointment and that the total service usually would take you two hours, set that service up on your service time sheet for two hours and fifteen minutes. Double-book as you normally would—that little extra time will help quite a lot.

Do not be afraid of clients' reactions when you start double booking. There is no doubt that clients will notice the change, and a few may initially resent the lack of your full attention. However, my experience has shown that clients are generally supportive, particularly if they recognize you as a professional in high demand.

Think about this in the big picture. Even if a few clients actually leave you because of the new practice, you will have room for a few new clients who won't begrudge you an opportunity to advance your business. It's all attitude and mind-set. I'll say this several times in this book: there is one of you and hundreds of them. You need to own this idea without becoming arrogant or taking your clients for granted. The moment you like yourself that much, there won't be hundreds of them any more. The confident professional hairdresser thrives; the cocky hairdresser starves.

If you doubt the value of double-booking appointments, consider the economic advantages. To understand this point, we will look at a second example related to double booking using the same clients from our earlier example.

Illustration two: Sue Jones is back at three o'clock for another appointment. This time, she would like a color, a haircut, and a style. She simply wants to take care of her gray new growth. The appointment will take a total of two hours. The color will cost her sixty dollars and the haircut will cost her forty. When we divide one hundred dollars by two (two hours), we find that our hourly income is fifty dollars. For a full ten-hour day, you would earn as much as five hundred dollars—a very respectable wage. However, by double booking, you can dramatically increase your income during that same ten-hour day.

(Yeah, I said ten-hour day. Make no mistakes: if you want to be successful in this business, you will work long hours. After you have "made it," you will find ways to relax and scale back a bit. For now, though, you work hard!)

At three fifteen, you finish applying color to Sue Jones's hair. While she is processing, you start a haircut on Pam Smith, who arrives for her three-fifteen appointment. The work on both guests is completed within two hours. You receive one hundred dollars from Sue Jones for the color, cut, and style and forty dollars from Pam Smith for the haircut. The combined total from both clients is one hundred forty dollars. Divide one hundred forty by two (two hours) to arrive at an hourly income of seventy dollars.

Now, let us suppose that you are double booking throughout each ten-hour workday. At an hourly average of seventy dollars, you just earned seven hundred (instead of five hundred) for the day. Double booking represents an additional two hundred dollars for the day, one thousand dollars for the week, and an extra fifty-two thousand dollars for the year. You will not just make fifty-two thousand dollars in income a year. You will make an additional fifty-two thousand dollars a year on top of what you were already making. Hello—anyone home? If these dollars don't give you enough reason to double book, then your interest in this industry is a vocational, not vocational. That means it's a hobby for you, Betty Lu, and this business is not a hobby.

Your earning power. Knowing what you're making on an hourly basis is essential if you expect to aggressively see this business in the big-picture sense. It is also helpful to know how much a client is worth to you on an annual basis. I don't mean that in a cold way; I mean it in a business way. Once you establish a good clientele base, your weekly and monthly tracking will allow you to figure out how much the average client means to you in annual business. This number is important for many reasons, but for me one reason stands out more than the rest. By knowing that number, I always knew what losing or gaining one client meant. I always knew what one mistake would cost me, and I knew what the efforts of gaining one new client were really worth. It's very difficult to take your clients for granted in any way when you know this.

This brings us to the bottom line—annual income and the potential you have as a successful hairdresser. Isn't that why you're reading this book? To earn a respectable income, you need only three clients each workday. That's right! You could earn over forty-eight thousand dollars a year a year if you did a perm (eighty dollars), a haircut (forty dollars), and a color service (sixty-five dollars) each business day of the year. This is gross income before taxes and business expenses. This estimate assumes a five-day workweek for fifty-two weeks each year.

I have a question: Can you see yourself handling more than three clients a day? I hope the wheels are turning.

Few hairdressers, however, maintain such an ideal client service load. In fact, none of us do. Furthermore, the cost of doing business and paying taxes will decrease your potential earning power. So you ultimately need to book more than three clients a day. Besides, why would you want to limit your earning ability to forty-eight thousand per year? The brass ring is there for you to grab, but you must put in the hours, build your business with conscious and deliberate effort, and avoid slacking off and getting lazy. It's as simple as that.

As you build, you will need to raise your prices. I have never met a hairdresser who looks forward to doing this, but it will have to be done. Get over it. Everyone knows that you run a business. Everyone knows that you have expenses. Everyone knows that prices go up. So why should it be any different in the hair industry? The answer is that it's not.

As you apply the concepts and tools explained in this book, you will get busy—really busy. You will get to a point where even though you're double booking and using an assistant, you find it difficult to get appointment times for new and even current clients. When it gets like that, it's time to raise your prices.

I won't try to go into too much depth on this subject; I will instead be very direct and tell you what has always worked for me. It's up to you to trust and follow the advice or to decide to reinvent the wheel. When you raise your prices, do not apologize—ever! If you apologize or give your clients any sense that you are not comfortable with the new prices, they will feel it—and they'll feel you don't deserve it.

Think about your dentist. You go in for your examination and you receive your service. As you check out at the desk, you notice the price has gone up by twenty dollars from the last time. Did your dentist apologize for the increase? Did your dentist send you a nice let-ter telling you the increase would take place as of a certain date? No! It's just the new price, plain and simple. If you happen to question your dentist about the increase, he or she would probably explain that expenses have increased and that the increase was necessary. You will do the same.

When you increase your prices, an amaz-ing thing happens: you lose a small per-centage of your clientele. Yeah, I said amazing thing because that's OK. You want this to happen. Remember why you decided to implement the increase in the first place? You were too busy to get people on your schedule. This may sound a bit cold, but a price increase will thin out your clientele a bit to allow new people—people who are willing to pay your new prices—to get on your schedule. Again, it's all about the attitude and mind-set that allows the business side of your brain to make the right decisions.

"What about my really nice clients who have been coming to me for a long time? They can't afford my new prices." As impersonal as it sounds, the business has to grow first. You have to make a decision to succeed and stick to it. Besides, as you thin out your clientele now and then, you will effectively help the other stylists in the salon by recommending clients to them and helping your clients stay in the price range that best suits them. Don't be surprised, though, when the clients who've left you find the few extra dollars to come back to you after they've had a few appointments with other stylists. Either way, your business grows.

When you set goals for yourself, make them realistic and use the concepts in this manual to drive your business. Revise your goals periodically. At times, you will find it appropriate to raise your goals; at other times, you may find it necessary to lower them. Remember that goals are targets—they are based on reasonable estimates of our personal skills and abilities. Sometimes we overestimate our skills and abilities; other times, we underestimate our potential. The most important thing is to stay active and involved in your business's growth; don't let this business "happen" to you. Be in control, and be intentional in your efforts.

To monitor whether or not you're attaining your goals, track your income on a weekly basis. Keep your finger on the pulse of your business at all times. If someone should ask you what you make per hour, you'd better know the answer off the top of your head. With time and through studying the lessons in this book, you will reach your maximum earning power.

Professionalism

Professionalism! I know, you heard all about it in school. Yes, you do have to read this chapter, too. Well, it's time to review the concept again. Why? Because the subject is so important and professionalism is the key to success as a hairdresser. If you do not incorporate a professional attitude into the way you do business, I guarantee that your income will never rise to the top 1 percent of this industry. I also guarantee that you will fail to experience any significant growth as a hairdresser. The concept and practice is that important.

There are many ways to define professionalism. I will cover several key points that stand out in my mind, and, in my opinion, contribute significantly to a hairdresser's success (and to a hairdresser's demise if they're not practiced).

Being on time. How can you argue against punctuality? It is probably the most common unprofessional characteristic and the one that goes the furthest in driving away clients. Put this concept in perspective: You come in to work or back from lunch a little late now and then. Even if you don't do this all of the time, your clients will see you coming back to the salon late. You are on their time—the time they bought from you. Remember that when it comes to charging for our services, we charge mainly based on time. When you are late, your clients will think you have little regard for their time. At the very least, your clients will treat you the same way if it suits them. At the worst, they will be offended and look for another stylist who is professional and respects their time.

Contrast that scenario with this next example. You are running behind in your schedule because of the extra atten-tion you gave to a client earlier in the day. Maybe it was just her first time in and she happened to have a lot of hair. Regardless, your client comes in on time and sees you working into her scheduled appointment slot. You see her looking at her watch, and you know you still have about fifteen minutes before you will be done with your current guest.

This needs to be a standard policy: Anytime you are running even five minutes behind, stop what you are doing and walk out front to let your next client know about the situation. If you do this, you will diffuse your next client's irritation before it happens. This will work 90 percent of the time if you make a point to talk to your client personally. Now I said personally. Don't send your assistant or the receptionist out to talk to her. You do it. Don't you want to know if she's upset? Who will be able to gauge her reaction better than you? Take care of it yourself. Besides, you're the one who needs to apologize for running late.

In the first case, the tardiness is unprofessional and establishes a barrier between the hairdresser and the client. In the second, the waiting guest accepts your attention to the client in the chair and appreciates the fact that you are giving her the attention she is paying for. Your waiting client also knows that she will receive the same attention when it's her turn to sit down.

Being on time is important to the client and should be important to you. Sometimes, the second scenario cannot be avoided; however, you should avoid being late for work at all times. Being late to work or coming back from lunch late speaks volumes about your priorities and tells the client how little you care about her time. If you do this even only on a semi regular basis, how do you think your clients will view you? Remember that you're always on stage and that you're selling an image. Make sure you're selling the right one. Evaluate your punctuality. If you have been late to work more than two times in the last year, you're late too often. No excuses! This is your business. It will thrive or die by what you do.

Shuffling Appointments. Shuffling appointments is a terrible habit to adopt; unfortunately, it's one that many hairdressers have. Shuffling is when you reschedule a client to a different time slot to accommodate your personal schedule. Few habits do more to remove the personal touch from our business than this one. It shows no regard for your clients' schedules, and it marks you with a reputation that is very hard to shake.

One of my staff told me once that he heard me say, "There's one of you and hundreds of them," and that's why he felt it was OK to engage in this practice. Firstly, I do say that. Secondly, that is not what I meant! That attitude of subtle confidence does not give you license to treat your clients like pieces of meat. Remember that each appointment is for a real person who will have a perception and an image of you whether you like it or not. You had better make sure you put across the correct perception all of the time.

Save moving appointments for true emergencies. Remember that you are in the service industry and are on demand for the convenience of customers— schedule permitting.

If you shuffle appointments, stop! If you do it infrequently, it better be for a good reason.

Combs and brushes. This one is simple. If you drop combs or brushes during a service, do not pick them up and use them on a guest. Just don't do it! Make a show of selecting a clean comb or brush from your station. If you're down to your last clean one and you drop it, run to the back and wash it. Who cares if you're running late and don't have time to wash it? Do you have time to lose the client? Do you really know your client so well that you are sure a dirty comb put back into her hair would not gross her out? Maybe you do know her that well. What about the client waiting in the reception area who saw you do it? Do you know her that well? You're on stage! They're watching! Maybe it's just better not to take the chance and to be a professional. A professional would not do that, plain and simple. If you want to be viewed as a professional, then it's a total package. It means that everything you do is at a different level.

What about cleaning brushes and combs? Do we need to discuss this point? Clean them! Once you have cleaned them, clean them again! Never underestimate the power of a clean comb or brush, and do not make the mistake of thinking a client will not notice a soiled or "used" brush. I can personally think of ten clients who came to me because their previous hairdressers used combs and brushes that were dirty or had other people's hair in them. They notice! Those clients didn't tell their last hairdressers why they left them—they just left. I'm sure those ten clients weren't the only ones who left their stylists for that reason; those were just ten who happened to tell me about it.

The solution to this problem is to buy a good number of combs and brushes and to clean them all before you leave for the day so they are ready for use the next day. Use some common sense.

Relocating. Hairdressers complain incessantly that moving from salon to salon disrupts their clientele. Why is it done then? Maybe because we can truly control our schedules, we feel that should translate to our being able to move to another salon whenever the mood strikes us. I don't know—I've never been able to figure out the rationale behind it. Who cares? It's bad business! Don't do it unless you really need to. Better said, don't do it unless you have a legitimate business reason to make the move. I had a stylist tell me she was leaving one of my salons because she personally didn't like the music we played. Wow—OK. Think with your head, not with your emotions.

Making a move to another salon should be a serious decision that you make for the right reasons. On average, hairdressers can count on losing 5–15 percent of their clientele each time they move to another salon. This average holds true for very close moves, but it's much worse if you move far away. Let's just say I worked at a salon that had another salon right next door to it. Let's say I wanted to move there—right next door. I would still lose 5–15 percent of my clientele if I made that move.

Why, you ask? People don't like change. They like routine, and they like their comfort zones. Take that away from them and you give them a reason to make a change themselves. Who knows—maybe you were late once or twice. If you move too, that could be just the reason a client needed to try the hairdresser that her sister has been talking about. She could move for a million reasons. The important thing to know is that it happens—no matter what. So don't do it unless you really have to.

Think about what a 5–15 percent decrease in business would mean. Let's say for example that you worked very hard over the last six months to increase your business by a total of 10 percent. By making the move to another salon, you have effectively set yourself back six months. The point is this: think everything through before you do it, and use your head, not your emotions.

Sometimes moves are unavoidable. A salon that is no longer able to provide a clean, friendly, professional atmosphere may interfere with your ability to build your business. In that case, moving may be your only option. Before you move, however, try to work things out with salon management. Make sure that a move is your last option.

If you do need to make a move, do it in a professional way. Send a nice letter or e-mail to every one of your clients. I have provided a sample letter that I've used in the past.

(Date)

To my clients:

I'm very excited to tell you about the opening of a new salon, (name of salon).

I have found the perfect environment in which to cater to my clients' every need and to pamper them "until they can't stand it anymore."

(Name of salon) will provide you with complete hair, nail, skin, and body care in a setting I guarantee you will love.

The salon offers complimentary makeup touch-ups after every service, as well as wine, soft drinks, and a variety of snacks.

As of (arrival date), I will be at (name of salon). There will be no changes to any previously booked appointments. All of my prices will remain the same as well.

A move to (name of salon) is a great move for my clients!

Your opinion is greatly valued. Please feel free to contact me with any thoughts or concerns prior to (deadline date) at (telephone number).

The shop is truly spectacular in its design and look. I look forward to seeing you at your next appointment.

Sincerely,

Alan Daniels   (Name of salon)

                                            (Address/phone Number)

                                            (Website/e-mail address)

Conversation: Hairdressers depend on conversation both for sanity and success. If you do not engage your clients in talk, prepare for a boring, unsuccessful, and short career. The topics we include in our conversations and the contexts in which we include them say a lot about our professionalism. One word of caution: use common sense and avoid conversations about religion, politics, and sex.

Obviously, we don't always follow that advise. The nature of our business allows us to become close to our guests. Its actually good business to allow that closeness to occur, as long as we don't "cross the line." By "crossing the line" I mean that we are the one who is dictating a conversation on a touchy subject. If you and your client are discussing a touchy subject, make sure that your client, not you, is advancing the subject. If your guest wants to tell you about her love life, you should allow that and take it for the compliment that it is. It does not mean that on the following appointment you get to share the details of your own love life! Don't do it! That's crossing the line of professionalism.

One final word of caution: Do not share your personal problems with your clients! You are there for them. It is their time, not yours. Burdening your client with your personal woes violates all professional boundaries. Besides, no matter how well you know your client, she doesn't want to hear it! She is with you for a service, not to act as a therapist for you. Our clients vent to us—not the other way around. Your client is paying you; it's his or her time. You have two ears and one mouth—use them appropriately.

When money changes hands, you are involved in a business transaction. That places business first in the relationship. When personal affiliations transcend the business relationship, the person in the chair ceases to be a client and becomes a friend. It's difficult to charge a friend for services or to increase prices for a friend. If you allow a client to become a friend, he or she will always lose professional respect for you. Always—they just won't tell you.

Sweep. Sweeping is a simple concept—do it, and do it often! Do not take a guest to a dirty workstation. It doesn't matter how far behind you currently are or how long your client has been waiting; don't take him or her back to a dirty workstation! This is about establishing a professional reputation. If your station is dirty, the client will perceive it as laziness, and she would be right! The combination of laziness and a dirty workstation says "unprofessional," plain and simple. Don't be that hairdresser; there are enough of them out there. You don't need to join that club.

Set yourself apart. Every hairdresser I have ever really talked to complains about a pervasive unprofessional attitude in our industry. Regrettably, it's a legitimate complaint. Ask yourself these questions: Are hairdressers looked at as professionals in general? Are we in the same professional category as, say, a pharmacist or a banker? If the answer is no, why is that? I submit to you that we—hairdressers—are to blame.

A vast majority of hairdressers fail to treat their training as a serious career move, and their clients know it. Many hairdressers get into this industry the wrong way and for the wrong reasons. They finish high school, and their parents tell them to go to college or get a job. They don't want to do either, so they go to hair school. They never looked at this industry as a serious career option. That is why we have such an industry-wide reputation for unprofessionalism.

While the industry at large suffers, you can benefit from this. This pervading lack of professionalism will allow you to stand out from the crowd in contrast. Regard professionalism as your credo. In a business that thrives for a professional perspective, you can become a major player. Very few hairdressers actually treat this industry as a business and intentionally employ business principles that will help them grow and succeed. Will you? All it takes is a decision and a deep resolve.

If you are perceived of as a professional, your reputation will grow. The more your reputation grows, the more you will be in contrast to the vast majority of the industry. Make the decision and the commitment to be seen in only a professional light, and you will succeed in separating yourself from roughly 98 percent of your peers. Nothing makes success easier than setting yourself apart from the crowd.

The Assistant Advantage

Maximizing your time is essential to expanding your client base, and one of the easiest ways to maximize your time is to acquire the help of an assistant/intern. To help you acquire and develop an ambitious assistant, I have prepared the following list of tips.

When to get an assistant/intern. An ambitious assistant is an asset when you want or need to double-book clients on a regular basis (see the chapter on double-booking). If you are unable to keep an assistant busy by yourself, get together with another stylist in your salon and share an assistant. Remember that the presence of an assistant should increase your hourly income. If your assistant doesn't allow you to keep a heavier schedule or help you to manage your clientele more smoothly, then you don't need one yet. An assistant isn't a luxury item that you acquire to so you can relax more. An assistant/intern is a tool to make you more money and to provide a higher level of customer service to your guests as you get busier.

Where to find an assistant/intern. During my years in the industry, I have always found it an easy task to locate and employ an ambitious and hardworking assistant. Firstly let me say that you need to know your state board's rules regarding assistants. Know what they are and are not allowed to do in the state you're in.

I always inquire first at local beauty schools; check with private beauty schools and university or junior college cosmetology programs. Contact the school's program director and let him or her know that you are seeking to employ a current or recently graduated student who is looking for an opportunity to apprentice. Don't rule out a current student as an assistant. There may be many things a current student can do to help you that does not violate any state board regulations.

Schools are generally cooperative and will locate work for their students, so do not be surprised if you receive a list with the names of several candidates. As an alternative to school programs, place an online ad to advertise for your assistant position. Use social media sites to advertise for an intern. The public may wonder why you are so busy that you need an assistant; that's a good thing.

Paying your assistant/intern. The wage you pay an assistant (if you pay at all) is entirely up to you. Remember this: You need to give something other than money to your assistant. The whole reason someone would take a position like this is the education and hands-on experience he or she would receive. You can pay your interns with money, but you had better pay them with education too, or they will quickly develop the attitude that they are just there to help you make money. If they develop that attitude, it will all go downhill from there.

The whole assistant arrangement needs to be very beneficial to both of you. You need to make sure that by paying your assistant, you are able to produce more income for yourself. Your assistant needs to feel that he or she is constantly learning and getting more familiar with life in a salon. She should know that the experiences she is getting are the direct result of the opportunity you gave to her. It is your responsibility to make sure that the relationship between you and your assistant goes down this road and doesn't veer off into a situation that is one sided.

When you engage an assistant, you must make sure that there is a clear understanding of what is expected from both of you. Talk about money last because money is simply a byproduct of the position; it's not the goal of the position. The goal of the position for your intern should be to gain experience that will allow him or her to acquire and build his or her own clientele. Your goal is to train and "grow" an intern who will one day be able to handle your overflow clients—to train a future stylist who all of your clients will already be familiar and comfortable with.

(By the way, I believe it is your responsibility to pass on what you have learned. You need to leave this business in better shape than you found it in, and you can do that by teaching others and sharing your knowledge.)

Providing compensation may serve as an incentive for the ambitious assistant, but it will never take the place of education and experience (unless you have an assistant who has no desire to be a stylist). When you have your talk with your future intern, you need to get a few facts straight. Firstly, interns are there to help you make more money and to help you manage your clientele more smoothly. Secondly, you understand that they are also there to acquire the skills to become successful hairdressers, and you will help them do that. Thirdly, education has value—particularly the education you will be giving them. This will not be a high-paying hourly job; part of the "cost" of their education will be to work at a lower rate initially until their presence helps you produce more income. Reassure them that in the end, if they really want it, you will turn them into successful and independent hair stylists—that's the payoff for them.

I have always paid my interns in two simple ways. The first is called "piecework." It simply goes like this: You will set a standard rate for individual services that they will do, and you will pay them only for those. For example, you might pay one dollar for a shampoo, five dollars to apply and rinse a color, five dollars to apply and take down a perm, and so forth. Your intern will keep track of everything he or she does for you, and you will pay him or her at the end of each day or at the end of the week. This is also a great system to use when an intern is being shared between two or more stylists. The intern will stay busy and will be paid based on what he or she helped you with. Obviously you can change the rates of each service as you see fit or value other forms of help—you decide.

The second pay compensation system I have used is a simple hourly rate. I would always use a low base hourly rate and simply "tip out" my interns a bit extra at the end of each day. This tip out would be based on how much the assistant physically did for me that day and also on how much the assistant went out of his or her way to make sure things went smoothly. I placed a lot of value on the personal attention my interns gave to my clients when they were caring for them. I would tip out or reward my assistants for showing the kind of attitude and attention to my guests that I would show them. Essentially, I reinforced the kind of behavior that they would need to be successful, which was part of the education I promised.

Utilizing the assistant/intern. An assistant has two main functions: to help you maximize your time so you can earn more money, and to care for and pamper your clients when you are with someone else.

If your assistant is not performing the second function well, reevaluate his or her use to you. More importantly, determine whether he or she is performing just as you taught him or her. Make caring for your clients your assistant's number one priority. Remember that when your clients are happy, economic prosperity will follow.

In return for teaching, experience, and compensation, I demand a lot from my assistants, and you should do the same. Doing the job alone is simply not good enough. You need to make them see that they are hair stylists that just happen to be in an assistant position. That means that they should act like they are hair stylists—now.

I make a point of expecting my interns to cultivate relationships with my clients. They are expected to get to know them and to engage in conversation with them just as I would do. You're supposed to be training them to ultimately become stylists, right? Isn't that what a stylist does? Then set standards for personality as well as for technical ability. Let them know that you will randomly ask them questions about a client that they've helped with and that they'd better know the answers. Expecting these intangible skills is part of the education you will promise. In short, the assistant should be everything you are to your clients, and that's exactly how you should train him or her to be.

One last thought on employing an assistant: Beware of the "greed factor." An assistant is an assistant, not a replacement for you. Never let an assistant do your job for you. The client is paying for your time and your experience, not the experience of an intern or trainee. It's very easy to become very comfortable with an assistant. It's very tempting to use an assistant more than you should—especially when more money is coming in because of his or her help. Don't forget your humble beginnings and what got you to where you are now. Don't get greedy.

For example, always walk over and physically check your own chemicals. You may be sure that it is time to shampoo off a color, and you may know that you don't need to check it to find that out, but walk over and check it anyway. Your guests need to see *you* do it. They need to know that you are handling their services and that they weren't simply handed off to your intern for the better part of an hour. If you don't personally check your own chemicals, you will send the message that what you do really isn't that difficult; after all, your intern applied the color, checked it, and decided when to shampoo it off. What does your client pay you for? Check it yourself!

Now there is one exception that would cause me to allow my intern to do a portion of my work for me. Let's suppose that a regular client of mine called in to the salon at the last minute and really needed to get on the schedule for a haircut and style. Let's suppose I am completely booked and can't fit her in anywhere except for in a twenty-minute slot that I have open. That's not enough time to give her a full haircut and style, so I might say something like, "I can get you in for a haircut only, but Michael, my intern, would have to style your hair for me. Is that OK?" In this case, Michael, the intern, would be helping me do a big favor for a regular client, so I would allow the service to happen this way. Now this would only happen if I were very comfortable with Michael's styling abilities. If Michael weren't ready to style one of my guests, I would never offer him up. You get the idea, right?

Now in the example above, would you give the client a discount of some kind because you had your intern style her for you? Of course not! The appointment was still with you. In fact, I would actually let Michael know how I wanted it styled just so the client knew with whom she had an appointment. Get it?

Most clients will accept the fact that a professional assistant is aiding you— they will regard it as a sign that their hairdresser is successful and in high demand. This is a good thing. You will have, in some cases, clients who resent your intern. These clients want all of your attention and will not accept your use of an assistant.

Let me be very direct about this: Just as with the concept of double-booking, you cannot allow a small percentage of your clientele to hold you "hostage" when it comes to building your business and making a life for yourself! You will never make all of the people happy. Try to make the most people happy while advancing your business. If a client ever puts you in a position where you need to make a choice between advancing your business and her as a client, ask yourself what will happen if you can't make your mortgage or car payment some month. Will your client make it for you? If the answer is no, feel good about making the hard decision and letting the client go. Do it professionally, but let him or her go.

Department Stores

Need clients? Visit a department store. I have always found department stores to be a great place to "rustle up" new clientele if you are ambitious and unafraid. Test this observation. Visit a local department store and walk through the cosmetics section—the shoppers you see and the sales staff behind the counters represent a potential client pool. I have built my trade around this discovery, increasing my clientele base by 40 percent through promotional programs at department stores. To do the same, you merely need a few pointers.

The first step is to target local stores with access to your salon. You want to select local stores to make your services marketable, attractive, and convenient for the shoppers you approach. If you are lucky enough to have several different department stores in your local area, choose the ones that cater to a more affluent clientele. Why? Because it is more likely that these shoppers can afford your services, and your association with an affluent department store will complement your professional reputation. Stores like Nordstrom, Saks, and Macy's are synonymous with professionalism and customer service. Make their reputation yours.

First contact. Once you choose a department store for a promotional program, you need to consider which service department will suit your purposes. I suggest working with the cosmetics department, which is what I have always done. Promotions in these departments are the most successful.

Call or visit to learn the name of the cosmetics department manager. Visit in person to meet with the manager, but make an appointment if possible. Don't just drop in—nobody likes that. When you get the opportunity, introduce yourself and briefly discuss your promotional concept. Allow the manager the courtesy of offering her own ideas.

Be prepared to accept responsibility for coordinating the promotional event—after all, it's your idea. If the cosmetics manager assumes that she or the store will have to shoulder the burden of staging and organizing the event, the answer may be no. Assure her that you will handle all of the organization and report often and directly to her. Don't make another job for the cosmetics manager; she usually has enough to do.

Each cosmetic line will usually have a counter manager just for that line. The counter manager is responsible for everything that happens at that counter. The counter manager will be very helpful in making sure the promotion succeeds; after all, it's her cosmetic line.

The idea. Coordinate a promotional event that brings in existing cosmetic department customers and also draws new customers to the event that happens to be walking through the cosmetic department. Make contact with and give consultations to as many of those customers as possible while making sure the cosmetic lines increase their sales; this will ensure they invite you back in for future events. The goal of all contact with customers and consultations is to schedule new appointments directly from the event.

A simple event would look something like this: The cosmetic line sets up appointments, they suggest and apply skin and makeup products, and when they finish the customer receives a five- to seven-minute hair "touch-up" and consultation. After the customer's time with you, you pick up your cell phone and call the salon to schedule her appointment with you. (Don't worry—we will go into detail about how to make this all happen.)

Making the promotion work. The promotion will require the cooperation of all cosmetic lines involved. All cosmetic lines do regular promotions to launch new products or to introduce seasonal events. They are used to the idea. But you add a new dimension to the event— hair. Most people who attend a cosmetic event receive an application of useful products, purchase the ones that suit them best, and go home. The event you set up will truly be an "event."

Start by talking to the respective cosmetic counter managers to make sure they will start contacting their current customers either by mail or by e-mail. Suggest that the cosmetic line schedule appointments, not just allow people to walk in the day of the event. A scheduled appointment seems much more exclusive, and if people confirm their appointments it usually yields a higher amount of people who actually show up.

Ask the counter manager how many appointments they plan to schedule and how far apart they plan to schedule them. That will give you an indication of whether you will need help on the day of the event or whether you can do it alone. Hopefully, you will need help. No matter what the counter manager says, encourage her to schedule twice as many appointments as she was planning on scheduling. For example, if she says they plan on scheduling one appointment every thirty minutes, tell her to schedule two. She will be concerned that she will have people waiting and that they will not be able to handle that volume. Trust me when I tell you that only 50 percent of the scheduled appointments will actually show up, even if they confirm the appointments. If she books double, she will always have someone in the chairs and will eliminate downtime. A small note on scheduling appointments at the cosmetic counter:

You must check with the cosmetic counter several times prior to the event to make sure appointments are being scheduled. Nothing is worse than taking a day out of your schedule to go to an event just to find out you will be standing around all day. Remember that this is your event and you have to keep an eye on it.

(The goals of the event are to talk to as many people as possible, to give as many consultations and ideas as possible, and to schedule as many appointments directly from the event as possible. You can't do that if you have nobody to talk to.)

Promoting the promotion. Make the event something that women will want to come to—something they won't want to miss. Create something that will keep them at the event for at least three hours if possible. Here are some ideas of event attractions I have used in the past.

Engage a photographer. The photographer will offer to take photos of the customers after they have had all of their services done. Maybe they will even offer a free five-by-seven-inch photo. Why would they do that? Because the customers will have to pick up their free five by sevens at the photographer's studio, where the photographer will have the opportunity to sell them family packages for the holidays, wedding packages, and other packages. It gives the photographer the opportunity to expose customers to his or her services. It's also an opportunity to get a mailing address or an e-mail address for future photography promotions. A free five-by-seven photo is a small price to pay for exposure.

Engage a videographer. At these events, the customers often love their makeup but can never duplicate the application process at home. Have the videographer tape the application and sell the video file to the customer for ten dollars. The customer can watch it over and over again to ensure that she can duplicate what the makeup artist has done. The videographer can simply sell a digital file that costs nothing, and he or she can also get contact information for a new client base and for promoting future events. Everyone wins.

Engage a florist. Talk to a local florist and ask him or her to donate several arrangements for the event. Why would a florist do this? He or she would do this for the exposure to a new client base. (Getting the idea?) The arrangements will be situated very nicely all around the event so they are very visible. You can suggest a couple of different ideas to the florist. Either have a silent auction for each arrangement where customers can fill out a small card to enter their bid for the arrangements, or simply raffle each arrangement off. Either way, the customers will have to fill out information cards that the florist can use for future promotions. The florist can also put up some elegant signage letting customers know who provided the beautiful flowers. Hey, maybe they could even give each customer a free rose when she leaves the event—who knows? Use your imagination.

Bring one or two nail technicians. This one is easy and fits into the event very well. The nail technicians will simply do polish changes all day—no manicures. Just like you, they don't give away their services. They simply make the customers' nails look better while suggesting regular services that can be performed at the salon. Maybe the nail technician can offer a drawing for a free manicure and pedicure. They, like you, will actually schedule those appointments from the event using their cell phones. At the very least, the new customers will leave with some suggestions and a business card.

Hair. Each customer will receive a quick five- to seven-minute "touch-up" of her current style and a very detailed consultation. You will not have time to style every customer that attends the event. You must make sure that all of the cosmetic staff describes your part in the event as a touch-up and consultation. If they say the word style, customers will expect something bigger than you can give them that day. You don't want people to be disappointed when they finally get to see you. It's always better to promise less and deliver more. If you happen to have a slow time in the event and decide to do more on a customer, let it be your idea, not the customer's expectation. Besides, you are not there to give your services away for free. You are there to gain exposure to a new client base and to introduce your services. This will be a "numbers game" for you. The more people you talk to, the more appointments you will schedule.

So this might be what your event would look like when a customer schedules an appointment and attends.

The customer checks in at the cosmetic counter where she is welcomed and told about the event. The makeup artist lets the customer know that her skin product and makeup application will be videotaped and available to her at the end for ten dollars if she chooses to buy it. She explains the advantage of having the application available to watch over again. The makeup artist starts her consultation with the customer and goes through their entire procedure. (Incidentally, when people know there is a camera on them, they tend to listen more carefully. That is good for the cosmetic line when it comes to sales.)

After the makeup application, the customer is told about the floral arrangements displayed all around the event. She's told that she can either enter a silent bid for the arrangements or simply enter a raffle to win one. Either way, the emphasis is put on the florist in a casual, simple way.

Now the customer visits the nail technician for a quick polish change. During that time, the nail technician introduces the customer to other services that she offers at the salon. The customer fills out a small info card so she can enter a drawing for a free manicure and pedicure. The customer chooses a polish color and gets a fresh look for her nails.

Now the customer sits down with you. You introduce yourself and ask the guest if she has been told what you will be doing with her today. You need to make sure that the expectations are correct and that the customer is not expecting a full style from you. Even if she says that she understands what you will be doing, explain that you are essentially there to give guests several new ideas and to answer any questions they may have about their hair. While that is happening, you will give her current style a quick "touch-up." You explain the process because no matter how careful you are about making sure everyone knows exactly what you will and will not be providing on the day of the event, someone will always sit down in your chair and expect more than you can give that day. Handle this person by person to make sure there is no confusion. Nothing is worse than giving a bunch of great new ideas, finishing your "touch-up," and finding out your guest is upset because she was expecting to have her hair styled. If that happens, you can forget about scheduling an appointment for her at the salon. Handle this person-by-person right up front, and make sure everyone is on the same page. The idea is to underemphasize the "touch-up" and to overemphasize the consultation and the new ideas. Think about it: What will bring this woman into the salon? The amazing five- to seven-minute touch-up you did on what was probably a bad existing haircut or the several new cut and color ideas you gave to her? Which one of those should you emphasize?

Make sure you write down all of your suggestions for her on the back of your business card or salon brochure. If you use a brochure, be sure to write your name on the front of it. She should look at this as a prescription just for her. It should include details about changing her cut, texture, and color. Be sure to let your guest know that you can schedule that appointment at the salon for her right now. You have to be a little brave, but you know the old saying—fortune favors the bold. If she doesn't schedule an appointment on the spot, suggest she hold onto your suggestions and that she bring them in with her when she does come in to see you. Don't be arrogant, but be confident that you will see her again. I have had clients come into the salon for the first time with a "prescription" list of suggestions that I gave to them at an event over a year before.

Lastly, the customer will visit the photographer. There she will pose with her beautiful makeup, her fresh nails, and her touched-up hair. If two friends or a mother and daughter attend together, encourage them to sit for a photo together. Make the event an event.

Organizing the event will take some time and some legwork on your part. Be patient, and check your details. In the end, it's your event; make sure it goes off well for everyone. When it comes to how to actually work the event and get the most out of it, there are a few simple rules that I have learned through trial and error. I have had several events completely flop and waste everyone's time. I would spare you that if possible. Be creative, and use your imagination when you plan your own event— just don't try to reinvent the wheel.

The only goals of these events are getting exposure to new clients and scheduling new appointments. You are not there to style hair and give your services away for free. You are there to meet as many people as possible in the short time you are there and to give each of them three new ideas for his or her hair. Every person you talk to *will* receive three new ideas. Now considering you might talk to between fifty and one hundred people in a single day, the idea of coming up with three new ideas for every one of them might sound a little tough. You will be talking to one person at a time. You don't need to come up with hundreds of new ideas in a single day. You just need to come up with three new ideas for the person in the chair at the time. Many of the ideas you suggest may be similar. As long as the person sitting in the chair at the time receives three new ideas, you have accomplished your goal.

Ask to schedule her appointment. You have given her at least three new ideas for her hair, you have pointed out examples of your ideas, and you have shown her pictures of cuts and color ideas that you brought from the salon. You did all of this, and she is excited about your ideas, so schedule her appointment. That is what you are there for. When you notice that she is excited about your suggestions, simply say, "You know, I could schedule that appointment for you right now." Wait and see what she says. If she is interested, simply pull out your cell phone and schedule the appointment. If she says something like, "That sounds good. Maybe I'll call you in a week or two," you need to go into your prebooking script. (See the chapter on prebooking.) Write your new clients' appointments on the back of your business card just like you would in the salon. Let them know that you will confirm their appointments one day in advance. Fortune favors the bold! Don't be afraid to ask to schedule an appointment; that is why you are there.

Don't be concerned about the small role you will play in the event as a whole. Remember that your goals are to talk to and to give consultations to as many people as possible in the short time you have. Create an event that brings as many people as possible to all of the people involved. Everyone will win if the event is busy.

Be very, very conscious of how sales are going for the cosmetic line. If they do not sell more as a result of your event—well, you know the rest. Make sure there is another event in the future. The best way to make sure that happens is to make sure the cosmetic lines and the cosmetic department have an increase in sales because of the event. Ask them what you can do or change to make sure that happens for them. They should know that you are concerned and are willing to make changes for them so that happens.

When you are working one of these events, you need to remember that you are not in the salon and that the same rules do not apply. In the salon, you are focused on only one guest at a time. At the event, you must be focused on everyone. While giving your consultation, pause and say hello to people walking by. Ask them, "Are you next?" Try to get them to stop and find out what is happening. Direct them to the cosmetic counter to sign up. Be very animated and outgoing. In these events, you must remember that you truly are on stage. Act like it. Don't act like you're standing behind your chair in the salon; act like you are on a stage in front of hundreds of people. Your customer is your model for the day. The event is a show! As you're doing your touch-up on your guest, if you see someone watching, ask her to come over and watch; ask her if she has any questions. Be bold. If the cosmetic line sees that you are pulling people into the event from the regular crowd just standing and watching or walking by, will they want you back again? The worst thing you can do at these events is to be quiet and reserved. I've said it many times before; people buy confidence.

Get to know the cosmetic line staff. They are "superclients" to you. If you are thinking about giving away a free haircut or two, these are the people to give them to. If you get a high-profile cosmetic line employee as a regular client, she could potentially refer many clients to you. Just think about how many women she comes into contact with. Take care of these employees.

Never cut hair at an event. Use your imagination to make these events bigger and better for everyone, but don't give your services away. Besides, how many people can you actually talk to and consult with if you are spending thirty to forty-five minutes cutting one person's hair? Customers don't have the patience to watch a whole haircut anyway; they will just get bored and walk away.

Never eat or snack on anything at the site of the event. If you need something to eat, walk away from the event and then go right back. Don't bring that big "tub-o'-cola" back from the food court after your lunch. Have a simple water bottle hidden behind something to drink from if you are thirsty. Remember, everything should look clean and professional at all times. You are on stage, and nobody wants to see you eat chips on stage.

Keep in mind that other hairdressers will see what you are doing and want to copy your idea. They might even secure an event with the cosmetic department as well. The managers of the cosmetic department and the cosmetic lines will decide with whom they want to work in the future. Be reliable and professional at all costs, and they will choose to work with you.

Lastly, make certain to acknowledge and thank the store's staff for their participation in the event. Write letters of gratitude to the cosmetic department manager, and give copies to the sales staff and counter managers. If all goes well, they will eagerly invite you back for future events.

Professional Distance

Maintaining professional distance is absolutely essential if you are going to succeed as a hairdresser. What do I mean by professional distance? Quite simply, you must detach yourself both emotionally and physically from your clients. Aside from conversation, you are not involved in their personal lives, and, with the exception of their appointment times, you are not their friend. You are not a therapist, moralist, minister, sexologist, or medical adviser. You are a hairdresser who is there to cut, style, and otherwise provide a service that makes them feel and look better. The bottom line is this: the only relationship you should have with your guests is a business relationship. Any measure of crossing that line will cost you success in your business.

This idea of professional distance is a tough one when you consider the nature of our business. Over time we always get close to our clients. It's how the business is, and it's actually encouraged and beneficial to building a clientele. So how can it be good and bad at the same time? Besides, many times it is the client who initiates the closeness in the first place. What do you do about that? The answer is simple: It is the client's choice to pursue the personal relationship, not yours. Clients pay for our time and service, and if, during this time, they choose to divulge personal information to you, that is their choice. As with everything in our business, there is a balance, and you must keep it. You are there to provide a service, and, if required, an interested and understanding ear. That is all.

I shouldn't have to say this, but I feel that I would be remiss if I didn't at least say the words. It is never appropriate to date a client. Never. Ever. My mentor, Johnny Hernandez, told me a simple rule very early on in my career: "Never sleep where you eat." (Except he didn't use the word "sleep.") This was the foundation of my professional-distance training that I would receive from him.

(Now for the sake of full disclosure, I must admit that I met my wife in my first salon in California. She was a client of the salon, but she was not my client. She was the client of one of my stylists, and even though I did pull her phone number from the appointment book without her permission—which was very unethical, by the way—I did not date my own client. About the phone number: I only did that once, and this year we will celebrate our twentieth wedding anniversary.)

If you break the professional distance ethic by sharing your personal life with a client or by engaging one in conversation regarding your political, moral, or religious philosophies, you will lose sight of your business objectives and forget that your central goal is to build a healthy clientele base. If you cross this line, you will ultimately be looked upon as less professional, and your business will suffer for it.

Perception is everything in the beauty industry, and respect as a professional is your most valuable asset. Do not sacrifice the image you have worked hard to build. Do not allow yourself to become so comfortable with your guests that you forget what you are there for. Remember that the moment that money changes hands, it is a business transaction, and not a gift from a friend.

Consider, for a moment, professionals in other fields, like your doctor, dentist, or attorney. What image do they suggest in your mind? You probably regard them as consummate professionals. Has you doctor ever met you for a drink? Does your attorney tell you about his or her love life? Has your dentist ever asked your out on a date? In most cases, they keep professional distance because it's best for business. Why is professionalism so intrinsically linked to the job titles of these high-profile professionals? Is it because they have excellent earning potential? Is it because they are well educated? Is it because of the way they conduct themselves? They command professional respect from their clients because they maintain a strict business relationship. Consider this question: Would you allow a physician with whom you maintain a personal friendship to give you a thorough physical examination? Most people would not. Friendship violates professional respect. Remember that when money changes hands, it's business.

Professional distance is incredibly important to doctors, lawyers, dentists, and other professionals. Why would we not try to achieve the same goal in our industry? Are we any less important? Are only they allowed this benefit because of their higher education? If you happen to question your dentist about the increase, he or she would probably explain that expenses have increased and that the increase was necessary. You will do the same. The answer to these questions is a simple one—no. In terms of professional distance, the only difference between a doctor and a hairdresser is that the doctor has made a choice and a decision about where the line is. Hairdressers don't always worry about crossing that line with clients. Heck, a lot of times there is no line at all! You must make the decision to keep the distance and stay professional.

Isn't it true that hairdressers provide a service that is, in most cases, more personal than the service provided by a dentist? A doctor's office is clinical; visiting an attorney is serious business. We visit these professionals because personal circumstances require it. Visiting a hairdresser is a choice. A hair appointment is fun and enjoyable. It is our job to make it that way for our guests, but we are not their friends. That huge distinction must be kept.

It's difficult to argue for professional distance when the very nature of our business requires close physical contact. The service you pro-vide requires it, and the need to establish trust with the guests requires it too. The key is to not cross the line. The correct form of physical contact is essential. A professional greeting is essential to building our business. A warm handshake with good eye contact will let your guest know she is welcome and that you are happy to see her again.

Do not hug your client! A hug is a close, personal expression not meant for a business atmosphere. Does your doctor hug you? If you have a client who wants to hug you, allow it, but do not be the one who initiates it. That would be crossing the line. Remember the importance of maintaining a professional image. The last thing you want is to be known as the "touchy hairdresser." A reputation like that will get around in a bad way. As a man in the hair industry whose clientele is 98 percent women, I learned very early on that my best intentions to be friendly could easily be taken the wrong way. Keeping a distance was a great way to stay professional in the eyes of my clients.

Sometimes you will have a client who has been through something very difficult in her life. Maybe she has experienced a family death recently. When you greet her, take her hand in both of yours and keep your eye contact a little longer. Say what you feel you should say, but do not hug her. If she needs a hug, she will let you know. Let her hug you if that is what she needs, but that form of expression should be on her terms, not on yours. Do not initiate that.

Give your clients the personal touch, but do it with compromise. Be attentive, charming, interested, friendly, and humorous. Offer personal advice when asked. The client bought your time and should use it as he or she would like. Don't use their time to share your life because it makes you feel better. Remember to listen twice as much as you talk. God gave us two ears and one mouth for a reason. No matter how long you have known the client, no matter how comfortable you are with each other, the moment money changes hands it's business first. Maintain your professional distance.

Lunch Is for Wimps

Judging by the title of this chapter, you may well expect me to talk about attitude adjustment. Well, you're right. To begin with, you need to develop a new perspective about the concept of lunch. In the movie Wall Street the character Michael Douglas plays suggests, "lunch is for wimps." The Douglas character implies that high-powered people satiate their appetites with the consumption of power and the creation of wealth. Fueling their metabolism with food is an afterthought. This might seem like an extreme example, but you get the point, right?

I want to create in you an attitude that "real hairdressers" don't set aside valuable time to go for food! Don't get me wrong—I eat lunch; however, I never mark out a specific time on my appointment schedule for it. I take time for lunch when and if a break occurs. Getting that extra client in should be your priority. When you are out to lunch with coworkers, you won't be available to serve the walk-in guest who called for the last-minute appointment. Established lunch breaks can also interfere with the eager hairdresser's appointments when she's engaged in a heavy double-booked schedule. The way I see it, an hour break for a ten-dollar hamburger, soda, and French fries may end up costing me sixty to one hundred dollars.

The simple lesson is this: If you intend to serve a large clientele, you need to be in the salon and available during all business hours. Leisurely lunches with coworkers will build camaraderie, not a client base and a business. In the end, your coworkers will not pay your car payment or your mortgage. The clientele you worked tirelessly to build and maintain will do that for you. Once you reach a yearly income of over one hundred thousand dollars, you can start taking scheduled lunches—sometimes.

You may think that giving up lunch is asking too much. If you are committed to this business and are willing to make the sacrifices necessary to achieve success, then it's not. Maybe you're reading this as a stylist who has been in the industry awhile and is very used to scheduling out for lunch. Remember the old saying: "If you always do what you have always done, you will always get what you have always gotten."

Do not misunderstand the message in this chapter. This is not an admonishment to avoid lunch. After all, your body and mind need nourishment. However, instead of leaving the salon, pack a sack lunch and eat in the break room, or ask a coworker leaving for lunch to bring something back for you—that way, if clients call or come in, you will be available to take them. The point is that you cannot attend to business if you are away from the salon. As time goes on and your clientele becomes more "solid," you may be able to disregard this rule a little bit—but not in the beginning of your career. Until you reach your goal, you must make a commitment that everything you do will be all business.

Complete Makeover Demonstrations

Creating a dramatic change with a complete makeover will earn you the undying gratitude of your client. Makeovers are also an excellent business-promotion tool. One of the best ways to attract new client interest is to offer and give these makeovers in a public place. One word of advice: If you do not specialize in makeovers, you will need the help of an assistant or a makeup specialist for the demonstration. Only do what you do well. Don't try to push yourself too far for the sake of doing it all yourself. Remember that hair always takes the starring role, so don't worry about sharing the spotlight. The end goal is the important goal.

For a makeover to complement your guest, it should bring about a dramatic change. A client amazed with her makeover results will talk up your services to her friends, family members, and associates. At a minimum, the complete makeover should include a total change to the application of a client's makeup, a haircut, a new color, and a style that gives her an exciting new look. If possible, color chart the client to demonstrate the dramatic changes possible with new additions to her wardrobe.

Doing a makeover—or a series of makeovers—in a public setting can really make your clientele grow quickly. Think about the excitement it can create; excitement creates talk. The location of the demonstration is crucial to its success. I have had exceptional luck by staging my makeover demonstrations at local schools, including elementary and junior and senior high schools. To arrange your demonstrations, contact local schools and schedule a few minutes to talk to faculty advisors. These staff members often set up events for their faculty.

Let the faculty advisor know what you have in mind. Let the advisor know that you are a professional stylist who is trying to get his or her name out into the local community. Let the advisor know that you are willing to donate your time to an event of his or her choosing to show what you can do. You may even want to attend a staff meeting ahead of your event to choose one or two models for your makeover demonstration. In my experience, the positive response to these offers is amazing. Assure all involved that nothing will be done without their full knowledge and consent. Emphasize that there will be *no surprises*.

The best part about working with a local school faculty is that all of the staff members know each other. Once the word gets out that Susan and Rachael are both receiving a full makeover at the next staff meeting, you can be assured that your name will be known. And that's before the makeover even happens! After it's over, that school might as well be yours. These events can take a lot of planning but will generate an abundance of new clientele for years to come. They are definitely worth the time to set up and do! On a personal note, my best and most loyal clients over the years have come from the education field. Focus in on them for a solid chunk of your clientele.

When scheduling your demonstrations, use your imagination to select locations. I have done makeover demonstrations at local utility company offices (electric, water, and gas), city halls, administrative offices, hospitals, and local churches. I suggest that you consider any office employing a large number of people—especially a large number of female employees. I have also conducted demonstrations in homes for baby and wedding showers. The entertainment value of these demonstrations gave the showers a "party" flavor, earing the hostesses considerable praise. For that matter, consider makeover parties to demonstrate your work and makeup product lines. Ask your salon's product sales representatives for help and free makeup or product samples to give away at the event. Focus your demonstration events within a five- to ten-mile radius of your salon. These makeovers won't help you much if your salon is too far away. Anytime you provide a makeover demonstration, use a sign-in sheet for tracking attendance. Ask for the name and e-mail address of each attendee. Incorporate this information into your advertising database for future events and promotions you offer at your salon. I offer door prizes to attract attendees. These giveaways can be anything from hair or makeup packages to gift certificates for a free haircut. Use your imagination. Products can usually be obtained for free from product representatives.

Now for the real reason you are there at the demonstration to begin with! After you have completed the demonstration and people are all excited, announce very clearly that you will be available after the event for complimentary consultations for anyone who might just "want a few ideas." Keep it casual. The more consultations you do, the more new business you will generate. If your event is happening during salon business hours, let the receptionist know ahead of time that you will be calling in to schedule a lot of new appointments. Use your phone and schedule those new people right from the event. Don't wait for them to call—offer to set it up for them now! Make sure that after each consultation you make a few notes describing your ideas for that person on the back of your business card. At the very least, the potential new customer will take that home with her and look at it as a prescription that was made up just for her. You will work these events exactly the same as the department-show makeup events described in an earlier chapter.

The point is this: you must "hustle" up your clientele. This one idea is a perfect example of that concept. One hundred percent of the potential new clientele from this or from any other type of promotional event would never be in your chair if you didn't first go out there and get them. You must work to attain your clientele and actively build it by using this technique and others like it. There is too much competition out there for you to sit around and wait for the salon to "feed" you business.

If you do that, this will be a long and fruitless career for you. Frankly, there are enough hair-dressers out there hanging around the salon waiting to be fed. Don't be that person. There is a reason that most people don't survive financially in the hair business. That reason is that they don't, or won't, do what it takes. Make the decision to stand apart from the crowd, and follow through.

Free Services—Who To Give Them To

The gift of free services is a jealously protected right of hairdressers. I do not know any professional hairdresser who chooses to not extend this courtesy on occasion. There is, however, an art to this practice. To give away services without a specific reason or simply to be nice is unhealthy for your business. It is also financially unsound for your business and can create enmity among clients who didn't receive the same gift. There are essentially two different and distinct categories of people to give services away to; for each category, there are different advantages to and reasons for doing so.

It is vitally important that we take good care of the clients we currently have. You should have a standard policy of free bang trims in between all haircut appointments. Every customer you serve and every potential client you talk with should be aware of this policy. Do not schedule appointments for bang trims—simply let guests know that they should call the salon the day of and that you will do your best to get them in. Even if your schedule is full, make time for the client—the bang trim, plus a brief moment of pleasant conversation, should take you a maximum of two minutes. If you have a client in the chair at the time, explain that you'll just be a few minutes and make sure she knows that you'll do the same for her when she needs it. Most clients will understand and appreciate your commitment to service. In the end, remember that there is one of you and hundreds of them. This is the way it has to be. Don't stress about it.

Any guest who has been loyal to you for at least six months should receive a free haircut for her birthday. I do not mean that you should give a free haircut to clients who happen to show up on their birthdays; I mean that all loyal customers get a free cut around and because of their birthdays. Keep track of your clients' birthdays using data cards or your in-salon computer. When you complete the cut, let the client know that "today's haircut" is on you. Don't let the guest know in advance that the haircut will be free. It's much better if your gift is unexpected. If they come in for a color and a haircut, simply charge them only for the color and let them know that the haircut is on you. Say something like, "Happy birthday, and thanks for taking care of me." Usually the tip will be pretty good that day, for your information.

Take care of those special clients who refer a large number of new customers to you. These customers should get a free cut once in a while—it is the best way to say thank you and one of the surest ways to encourage them to continue to refer more customers to you.

I have a standard policy for loyal clients heading to the altar—on the day of their wedding I do their hairstyles for free. Again, do not tell them ahead of time that the style will be free. Surprise them after their service is done, and it will seem more like a gift and less like a customer service policy. For a significant "life moment" like a wedding, isn't that what you want?

When you extend free services to new clients, it is very important to carefully pick the people to give them to. You want customers that are high profile and are likely to refer a good amount of new business to you. High-profile customers include owners and managers of successful local businesses; operators of local health spas or gyms; the priests, pastors, or ministers of local churches; local politicians; sales people behind the cosmetic counters at upscale departments stores; university professors and administrators; and the heads of nursing staffs at local hospitals. Brainstorm—with a little thought, you can generate an extensive list of potential clients with highly public profiles. Your objective is to offer one free haircut to get the person in your chair. After that, all you have to do is apply the lessons learned in this manual to make them satisfied, loyal, and likely to refer you to others.

Do not be afraid to inform them that you expect them to refer new clients to you. Do it in a nice way, but let them know that the idea is for the two of you to help each other. People in high-profile positions often engage in this sort of "tit for tat." Give them a good supply of your business cards when they leave the salon and remind them to "put them to good use." When you see them next, ask them if they need more cards. This is a bit of a trick question—if they say "yes," give them more and thank them for referring clients to you. If they say they still have some, say something like, "You still have some? How am I suppose to build up my business if the cards stay in your purse?" As always, do this with humor, not with a serious tone. It will accomplish your goal and get them to start thinking about referring you.

Look at free services given as a long-term growth practice—they're an investment in your future. When you put it into perspective, you will realize that you are giving away only a little bit of time for a tremendous volume of goodwill and gratitude—but only if you choose those situations and people carefully and deliberately.

Incidentally, any service that is given away becomes a valid "promotional expense" and may be a deduction on your income taxes. Check with your CPA to be sure, but keep track of everything. Be certain to keep a separate file on your computer just for "promotional" giveaways. Record dates, times, services, and the names of clients who received free services. Retention of this information is absolutely necessary if you are required to provide proof of these expenses in the event of an IRS audit.

Business Cards

Business cards are your personal marketing and advertising department. Regrettably, most hairdressers give little thought to their use and design. When you hand out a business card to a potential new customer, it should make an impact. The card should give the impression that you are progressive and artistic. The card should say something about you. To achieve this, your card must set you apart from the standard hairdresser crowd; it should stand out visually in their purse, wallet, or business card file; it should remind the client of you.

If you are given a business card from the salon you are working for and it doesn't make the impact that you would like, ask them if they will allow you to design your own card. In the end, you may have to wait to do this until you are independent.

Since business cards are your marketing tool, you will want to pass them out often. This brings into play the issue of cost. Impressive multicolored business cards can be expensive. Check online for Internet-based companies to produce your cards for you. They will tend to be more competitive on pricing because they don't have the print shop overhead to contend with.

I know for a fact, however, that when you are out "hustling" new clients, a professionally designed and uniquely styled business card combined with your positive approach and attitude will make you stand out from the crowd. With that combination, I find that people take me more seriously than the average hairdresser, and that translates to appointments, which translates to money.

Don't go anywhere without your cards! I cannot stress enough the importance of having business cards with you at all times. You should look at every outing as a potential opportunity to acquire new clients. Each person you meet is a prospective client. Be ready to advertise yourself and your business by handing out business cards. If you are not constantly thinking about building your client base, and if you do not have business cards ready to pass out, then you are missing significant opportunities to market yourself. Take your cards with you!

Here is a trick I've used to effectively build my clientele base. Whenever you finish with a guest, make sure she leaves with at least four of your business cards—no less. Adopt the attitude that every client you work on lives the results. When guests appreciate the work you have done, they tell friends. If she does not have your cards to pass out, you may lose a chance to pick up new clients.

When the guest returns in five to six weeks (because you prebooked her, right?), ask her before she leaves if she still has your business cards with her. The question lets her know that you expect her to pass out your cards for you. If a client still has cards with her from her last visit, joke with her and say, "How am I going to be able to send my kids to college if those cards stay in your purse?" This is not done with any kind of serious tone. It's done with humor, but your guest will get the message that you expect her help. Have fun with this whole idea. Don't stress about it. Tell you clients to give your cards out to people with "ugly hair." Keep it light and funny, and that's how it will feel for both of you. After a while, you will build a culture within your clientele. Handing out business cards is simply something they will all do.

Above all, be consistent with all forms of marketing. Do not prejudge whom you will and will not give cards to. Marketing yourself is simply something that you do all of the time.

Before & After: A Photo Journey

If I had to choose one sales tool that seems to impress clients the most, it would have to be my before-and-after photo album. Guests cannot seem to get enough of it. Putting together a before-and-after album is a definite asset for your business. It gives you a certain degree of credibility from the start. Seeing that you created drastic changes for so many other people instills a sense of confidence in clients. In any event, it inspires them to think about their own look, making it easier for you to suggest makeover changes.

The first step in producing a before-and-after album is to purchase an inexpensive digital camera. This camera always stays at the salon. Each time you're about to make a decent change in a client's look, ask if she would mind if you took before-and-after photos to include in your album. When you take the "before" photo, ask your guest to look serious—no smiling. After you've completed the change and touched up her makeup, take two or three photos of her smiling. Make sure that when you print the photos for your album, you print the "after" photo twice as large as the "before" photo.

If the difference between the "serious" and "happy" photos bothers you or strikes you as misleading, remember that your objective is to show a dramatic change. You are simply using a common marketing practice to demonstrate the change that can come from a complete makeover with you. Taking photographs establishes the memory of the journey for each client.

After you have finished the service and have taken the photos of your client, offer to e-mail the before-and-after photos to her. She will inevitably forward them on to her friends, coworkers, and family. Make sure your contact information just "happens" to be at the bottom of the e-mail. Always marketing, right?

The Barter System

Bartering is the process of trading goods and services without the exchange of money. As an economic principle, bartering predates all known monetary systems; as a custom, it is practiced in almost every culture and enterprise. Within the beauty industry, bartering has failed to achieve widespread acceptance. The lack of bartering among hairdressers and their clients is ironic because we provide a service that almost every person needs.

When I purchase goods or services, I often think about the appropriateness of bartering. Large corporations and their board of directors make bartering almost nonexistent in retail stores. In today's global economy, it is in the service industry and with small private retailers that bartering is most common.

If you find yourself in a situation ripe for bartering, I suggest you consider it. After all, you really do have nothing to lose other than the investment of your time. If you do barter, practice it with some finesse; bartering is, above all, a civilized process with rules of decorum.

You are trained to provide a valuable service that people want and need. Respect yourself and what you have to offer. Suggest a trade of services with the attitude that you have something just as important to provide. Do not sell yourself or your services short. If you choose to barter, stop and consider exactly what your services and your time are worth and let that be your baseline when you barter.

How should you apply your bartering skills? Let's consider one example. You need business cards to promote your business. Suggest a bartering trade with your printer. You may be able to receive a supply of business cards by offering your services. Do not limit your bartering to the print shop owner—include his or her spouse and kids in the process if that will be beneficial to him or her. Once your printing needs are met, the printer and his or her family will be likely to remain with you as clients. This is just one example of a case where bartering might work well for both parties. Use your imagination, but don't sacrifice your professionalism.

Do not ignore the potential for bartering. Consider its use as another marketing device to increase your clientele base. Give bartering a try. You will not know the possibilities of the ancient trading principle until you do.

Scouting for Models

Every hairdresser has downtime—that period of time during regular business hours when his or her chair is empty. The fact that we have downtime is not necessarily negative. Use this time to build your clientele. I use downtime to visit a local mall and look for models. If a mall is not within your immediate area, visit any commercial area, church, sporting arena, park, or any other popular setting where people congregate in large numbers.

Scouting for models: When I scout for models, I walk up to a person I believe has potential, introduce my profession and myself, and ask if he or she would consider modeling for a fashion show. Now keep in mind that people are suspicious at times. As a male hairdresser, the first reaction I usually get from females is a questioning look that asks if I am attempting a "pickup." To allay these concerns, I immediately hand the person a business card and explain that I am putting together a fashion show and am looking for fresh new models. Mention the word "model" frequently; it is flattering, makes an impression, inspires a sense of success, and places the approach into a professional context.

Reassure the person that nothing will be done to her hair without her permission. Use the phrase, "I promise—no surprises." Tell her that you need to work with her hair prior to the fashion show to develop the look that best suits her. Make it clear that all work will be complimentary. With enthusiasm, tell her that you have some great ideas for her. At this point, you need to make physical contact with her. Reach up to gently touch her hair. Don't worry, you're a hairdresser—it's expected. Touching her hair will let you know what texture you're really going to be working with and will give you a better idea of what her hair is really capable of.

The magic touch. Touching someone's hair is appropriate professional conduct. When you talk to someone about his or her hair, always reach out and touch it. Touching hair does several important things. Firstly, it lets the person know that you are really thinking about her hair, not just talking about it. Secondly, it clearly establishes your professional demeanor and credibility; thirdly, it puts you in a position of control—touching someone's hair brings her into your world where you are the authority figure. Fourthly, it establishes contact on a personal level, and that is the key to a good business relationship.

(Side note: Never do a consultation without touching the person's hair. Not only are all of the points listed above true but, it's also true that when you touch a person's hair, he or she tends to really "hear" you and listen. If the client isn't listening, all the best suggestions in the world won't matter.)

Finalizing Arrangements. After you have made physical contact, ask the model for the necessary personal information—her name, her work number, and her cell phone number. Inform your model that you will contact her within the next week to schedule an appointment for a consultation. At the consultation, schedule a complimentary cut and style. Instead of using "complimentary," I prefer saying that the "cut and style are on me." This approach is more personal, and it lets her know that you are giving something up for her.

If you should happen to cancel the fashion show or change your mind about the model, follow up with her and offer the complimentary cut and style anyway. Chances are good that she will stay with you as a paying client. In the end, isn't that what this is all about? Isn't it about building your clientele in as many ways as possible?

Scouting for models is a promotional tool for business. Ethically, you should only be doing it if you are planning a show or a makeover demonstration. In the end, you may or may not use the person you contacted as a model. However, until you get her in your chair, you will never know if you can give her a look that will impress at a show. The key is to get her in the chair for the first time and to impress her with you abilities and manner. The rest will follow.

Promotions With Church Groups

Local churches and church-affiliated groups offer a number of opportunities for the ambitious hairdresser. These institutions are often open to any promotional ideas that benefit their congregations. Here is one example of a successful promotion.

In the vicinity of my first salon in California were several private Catholic schools. One, an all-girls Catholic school, hosted an annual mother-daughter lunch banquet. One feature of the banquet was a student fashion show. In past years, my staff and I volunteered to visit the school during the banquet to style the hair of the student models. The school faculty was eager to have our participation, and in return they allowed us to place our business cards on each banquet table. We also placed a placard sign at the entrance to the banquet room that identified our salon, its location, our website, and the services we offered.

At the first banquet we volunteered for, we were responsible for styling roughly ten to twelve students for the fashion show. All of those students were finished before the banquet began. We found ourselves killing a little time just watching the event, and we noticed an opportunity. In the banquet room we noticed a long line of mothers and daughters who were waiting to have their pictures taken. With nothing to do, we walked the line and offered to quickly "touch-up" the hair of each mother and daughter before they had their pictures taken. Their reactions were amazing. People were so happy and grateful for our offer. Some of the ladies actually got out of line and waited to have their hair done before having their pictures taken. It was a lot of fun, but we were there for business. We didn't want to waste an opportunity, so we made sure that each of the ladies who we "touched up" received three new ideas for her hair. We gave quick consultations to each person and made sure we wrote down those ideas on the back of our business cards so she could take the suggestions home with her. We "planted the seed" for new cuts, colors, highlights, and more. The amount of phone calls for new appointments that followed the event was incredible.

The school also offered a drawing to which we donated gift certificates for several free haircuts. I asked permission to get on the microphone and announce the winners of our gift certificates myself. They were happy to allow it. Think about it: Why let someone else give your services away? Don't be afraid—get up to the microphone and do it yourself! The crowd seemed to be pretty charged up, so I threw a few salon T-shirts out into the crowd toward the end. They loved it, and we did it while remaining professional and without taking over the event.

The event was so successful for us that we did it again year after year. In the following years, we brought our nail technician with us to give away free polish changes. She also gave consultations and received a lot of new clientele from the event.

The new business that this one event generated for us was huge, but no price could be put on the amount of goodwill and positive talk around the city that our volunteering created.

The point of this chapter is to illustrate a personal story that was very successful, but I also want to convey the idea that you need to take advantage of opportunity when it presents itself. The original idea for this event was to simply style the hair of the students who were in the fashion show. In the years that followed, we realized that all of our new business was coming from the time we spent doing the "touch-ups" in the photo line. That became the event for us! If we had only styled the fashion show models and left the event right after that, we would have missed out on the real opportunity.

Take the above example and apply it to any number of group gatherings that could potentially offer you the opportunity to expand your clientele base. Do not limit your selections to church groups. Use your imagination. Most organizations have large group gatherings that could offer opportunities for you to promote yourself and your salon.

Remember that getting out in public and showing what you can do is always ten times more effective than buying some advertisement. Think about it: If you only buy or create an add about yourself, all you're essentially saying is, "I'm good—really. Trust me." Get out into the public and show off. Stand back and say, "Yup, that's what I can do." Don't be afraid to get out there. It's good to be on stage. Don't sit on the sidelines. Make your name known in your community. It will set you apart from the rest in both reputation and income. If you don't do it, someone else will—I promise.

Networking In The Salon

What would you say if I told you there is a nearly complete clientele load waiting for someone to claim them? Interested? Well, there is, and this Land of Oz is right in your backyard, Dorothy. Where is this untapped reserve of clients? They are the customers of the other technicians—the nail technicians, makeup artists, estheticians, and massage therapists—in your salon.

Consider your nail technician for a moment. How many of his or her clients have had their hair done in your salon? Meet with the nail tech and make an assessment. That number is probably very low. Those people are getting their hair done somewhere; it might as well be with you. I imagine that they would like to have all of their beauty services done at the same location, so make it easy on them. Unfortunately, hairdressers are reluctant to approach the clients of other salon technicians. Do not be intimidated by the idea of moving ahead and making those clients yours. Recruiting those clients is OK—it's not taboo. But never solicit the client of another stylist—that wouldn't go over very well.

This brings up an interesting point. We all know that we don't try to "steal" clients away from our coworkers. That's crossing the line. But where is that line really? I have seen hairdressers refuse to do the hair of other stylists' clients even after the clients asked if they could schedule with them. They refused because they were afraid to offend a coworker or because they were afraid of how the other stylist might react. That's ridiculous. Let's look at it like this: A client wants to leave her existing stylist and go to you from now on. You say no for whatever reason. Now the client will leave the salon entirely, and none of you will have that business again. Ridiculous. What about the client? Doesn't she get to choose who she receives services from? Never turn down a client from another stylist. If a client asks to schedule with you, you do it. It's not "stealing" if the client requested you.

Approaching the nail/skin technician and her clients. Be direct in your approach. Ask the technician if you can talk to her clients about their hair-care needs. Offer an exchange with the technician. Suggest that in return for her client referrals, you will refer your clientele to her. If successful connections are made with technicians in your salon, you should soon see your clientele base expand significantly. You will also improve the working relationship between you and the technician. Make sure, though, that if you to them in return you deliver on that promise. Do not allow referrals to become lopsided on any one side. If that occurs, you may need to consider other forms of compensation such as the ones discussed in the subsection "Motivating the technician."

Setting goals and developing interest. You and the technicians should make a commitment to refer approximately two clients to each other each week. Talk to each other often and find out if the referrals you both are making are working. It may be necessary to develop client interest for the services of the salon technicians who are cooperating with you. If the other technician is a manicurist, for example, ask her to do a free polish change on each of your clients; if the technician is a makeup artist, ask her to lightly touch up your clients' makeup. If the technician is a massage therapist, ask her to give each of your clients a simple neck or hand massage. You get the idea, right? Little "teasers" of free services are very effective in generating interest.

Your part in this trade is to give free bang trims or other minor services including quick hairstyle touch-ups. The free services you offer should be no more than two to three minutes in length. While doing this, you should be giving a consultation to the prospective client and suggesting a minimum of three new ideas. Make sure that while you are emphasizing ideas for cuts and styles, you make sure to touch her hair.

Motivating the technician. Targeting the customers of other technicians in your salon is an excellent way to build clientele, and it involves very little effort on your part. If a technician is not keen on the idea, find out what you can do to motivate her. Consider offering her a fifty-dollar gift card from her favorite department store if she refers a set number of clients to you. Cash could be the incentive she needs; or, you may consider offering 50 percent of the profit you make on the referred client's first visit. Consider all available options to promote this concept with you salon's technicians.

Getting new clientele into your chair for the first time is the objective. Once you have the referral, the retention of the client is left to you. Give this networking recommendation a fair try, and don't forget to prebook as they leave.

Clientele Database

Keeping a current database of your clientele is essential to building and maintaining your business. A database is what allows us to keep track of every detail concerning our clients. Long gone are the days when you could simply rely on memory. Can you imagine how hard it would be to remember two hundred different color formulas? What about when Sue comes in to the salon and tells you that she likes the formula you used on her last summer the best, and you've adjusted that formula by a quarter of an ounce several times in the last year? Forget it—there is no way you could remember all of those details with accuracy. A mistake is guaranteed.

These days, a database is a must for the professional hairdresser. It's a tool like any other, and you will use it to build your business. Most salons will have computer software to manage appointments, keep track of sales, and give reports. All of these software programs have a feature that allows you to keep track of clientele. If the salon you work at does not have a computer system in place, purchase a simple laptop computer or use your smartphone to keep clientele details. It doesn't matter how you keep the technical information on each client—just make sure you keep it.

Keeping the detailed information about color formulas and even graduation angles of a cut is important. It helps us to stay consistent in our technical work. But staying consistent in our work is not the main thing that guests remember, and it's not the main reason they continue to come back. When it comes to customers giving repeat business to any service-based business, one factor stands above the rest: how the customer felt when he or she left. The decision of whether or not to give return business is oftentimes an emotional one, and in the hair industry, that couldn't be truer. Here is a good example.

Have you ever had the experience of a new client sitting down in your chair for the first time and telling you all about her life in the course of forty-five minutes? Most of us have. To the hairdresser, that new client may have simply been the third of twelve appointments for that day out, but you need to realize that to that new guest, she was the only appointment of the day. She told you all about her kids, the job her husband just lost, their sick dog, and her uncle's hip replacement. While she told you all of these details, you were interested and engaged her in conversation. Is there any reason for her to believe that you would not remember those details during her next appointment? Clients don't understand that hairdressers hear this detailed information all day long every day. Sometimes we see several hundred people in a month. That is our reality and our experience, not the reality and experience of our guests.

Get this into your head: You must look at things from your clients' perspectives at all times if you are going to be successful in this business. If you look at situations through your clients' eyes, you will always know what to do.

So now it's five weeks later, and Sue is back for her second appointment with you. She is eager to come back because she liked the cut you gave her and she really felt like she "clicked" with you. She's eager to start telling you "chapter two" of her life when you say, "So, Sue, do you have any kids?" She may not say, it but she's probably thinking, "Any kids? We talked about my kids for thirty minutes last time." This is bad, and you need to know that this happens every day in the salon but that we never hear about it because the client is usually embarrassed that we didn't remember and never says a word.

I have tried to illustrate the importance of this point to my staff for years. I have boasted to them that I could go anywhere in the country and build a clientele faster than any other stylist in the salon. I didn't say that because I was better or cooler than everyone else. I said it because for me, remembering the details of my clients' lives is paramount. I do it because I know that it's how they feel when they leave—and not the haircut—that keeps them coming back. I concentrate on what's in their head, not what's on it.

So how do you remember all of this information and use it to build your clientele? The clientele database! Every time I finish an appointment with a new client, I go to the computer and make notes about her. Simple notes like "married, teaches school, three kids, husband police officer, from New York." I purposely don't add too many details. I just want to remind myself of the basics of what she told me—the rest I'll remember as time goes on. Can you imagine how she would react if on her second appointment I started off by saying something like, "So, Sue, how are Billy, Timmy, and Johnny, whose birthdays are in January, February, and March, and how is your dog named Fido doing?" That would seem a bit fake, don't you think? The idea is to write down the basic information, check those notes before you bring her back to your chair, and use those notes to remind you of what you talked about the last time. She should feel that the two of you are just picking up where you left off the last time. After you get to know her, over time you won't need those notes, and the only time you'll write something new down in the database is when she shares something important with you that you don't want to forget.

Most salon appointment software programs will keep detailed records of all of your clients' appointments, how often clients come in, what they come in for, and clients who have not been in for a while. Use the database to reach out to these clients and to try to get them back again.

Hairdressers are so funny about clients who have left them. They tend to take it personally. Why? It was never personal. You didn't date, pick out curtains, or walk on the beach together. (At least you better not have!) So why do we feel like we've been "dumped" when a client goes to another stylist? The bigger question is, why don't we try to get those clients back after they've gone? Think about it. They're already gone, and they already no longer come to you; what do you have to lose by making an effort to get them back in your chair?

This is where your clientele database comes in very handy. Compile a list of guests that you have not seen in the last six months and get ready to send out a letter. I said a letter, not an e-mail. The personal way is the best way when it comes to reaching out to lost clients.

Because of the personal nature of our business, when a client leaves us and goes somewhere else, she will sometimes feel a bit guilty about "cheating" on us. Sometimes that little bit of guilt will stop them from coming back in to us even if they would like to come back. They are afraid of a stylist saying something like, "Who cut your hair? That's not my haircut." This little fear will oftentimes keep them away for good. That's not good for anyone. Sometimes in this situation all a client needs is an excuse to come back. Your letter will give her that excuse. I have included a sample letter on the following page that I've sent out many times during my career.

Alan Daniels, *for Style*

Summer is near, and that means looking your best. Since 1986, award-winning stylist Alan Daniels *has been creating hairstyles for women to help them achieve their true beauty.*

If you haven't been to Alan Daniels *lately, now is the time to come back. For a limited time only,* Alan Daniels *is offering returning clients a complimentary cut-and-style makeover, valued at (price). To qualify, make an appointment with* Alan Daniels *for your first cut and style and your following visit will be absolutely free. Additional style services are available for a modest cost.*

This offer is nontransferable, and your first appointment must be made by (deadline date—two months from when you send the letter). Bring this complimentary certificate with you to your first scheduled appointment.

*(Salon name) hours are Tuesday through Friday, 8:30 a.m. to 8:30 p.m., and Saturday, 8:00 a.m. to 5:00 p.m. To make your appointment, call (phone number). Tell the receptionist that your appointment is for the "*Alan Daniels *come-back offer."*

Your beauty is natural. Come back to Alan Daniels *for the style.*

Signature   *Salon Name*

                                                 Phone Number

Don't be afraid to "jazz" us your letter with graphics of some kind. Remember that there's nothing to lose. The value of maintaining a clientele database should be obvious now. The information collected serves as a useful reference tool and a valuable recourse for building a large clientele. Keep this database current and active. You will be surprised by how often it is relied on. The technology available today makes keeping your database very easy.Remember: It's how they feel when they leave that really matters. Use your database for it's most important application—to connect and stay connected with you clients.

Your Receptionist

Building a close professional relationship with your receptionist is essential to the development and maintenance of your business. Think about this statement for a moment. The receptionist is the first and last person your clients see when they come to you for their appointments. Apart from you, the receptionist is the person most involved in your business. Your receptionist is involved in many ways beyond greeting clients, talking to them, and booking their appointments. Should you establish a close business relationship with your receptionist? Absolutely!

This is one of those things you must do deliberately—whether or not you get along with her and whether or not you like her. Make it happen.

What does a business relationship with your receptionist entail? Firstly, you both need to have a clear understanding of what you need from each other. She has a job to do, and you have a business to run. Take the time to talk with the receptionist about what you each can do to make the other's job run more efficiently. If you do this with her interests in mind, I guarantee that it will make a lasting impression on her and that she will be more likely to look after your interests in return.

Explain to the receptionist exactly how to handle your clientele in different situations. Discuss guidelines for when to call you to the phone to talk to clients. Define exactly how you want appointments entered in your schedule; make your expectations easier to understand by writing down a complete list of all the services you provide, noting the cost and time required for each service. (See the "Service, Times, and Prices list" provided on next page.)

Service, Times, and Prices

Name:_____

Services	Time Allotted		Prices
Shampoo/Style	hr.	min.	$
"Updo"/Formal	hr.	min.	$
Haircut—Men	hr.	min.	$
Women	hr.	min.	$
Kids	hr.	min.	$
Bang Trim	hr.	min.	Free
Perm			
W/Haircut	hr.	min.	$
W/o Haircut	hr.	min.	$
Foil/Highlight			
W/Haircut	hr.	min.	$
W/o Haircut	hr.	min.	$
Perm Color			
W/Haircut	hr.	min.	$
W/o Haircut	hr.	min.	$
Semiperm Color			
W/Haircut	hr.	min.	$
W/o Haircut	hr.	min.	$

Double-Booking

Haircut _____minutes after Highlight

Haircut _____minutes after Perm Color

Be sure that you leave this sheet in a place where the receptionist can easily access it when she is scheduling appointments for you. Be correct with your times and try very hard not to run behind on your appointments. Adjust the service times on your sheet if necessary. Know that the receptionist will schedule your appointments based on the information you have provided.

It is your responsibility to check the appointment schedule often to make certain that appointments are booked correctly and without conflict. This is especially important as it relates to double-booking your clients. (See the section on double booking.) Your objective is to train the receptionist so that she can handle scheduling your appointments as you would. If in the end your books are not managed properly, it is your business that will suffer. Take responsibility, and be involved.

Now that you know what to expect from a receptionist, how do you get her to perform to those expectations? You need to remember that the receptionist is also responsible to other hairdressers. This is an important point. Be patient, and work persistently toward your goals; however, do not forget to consider the needs of the receptionist. Ask her often if there is anything you could be doing differently to make things easier on her. Remember her on her birthday and at Christmas. The simple rule is this: take care of her, and she'll take care of you.

In the first salon I opened, one of my stylists would give each receptionist a Christmas card every year with a very sincere thank you note and fifty dollars. He was a very smart person. The receptionists always seemed to go out of their way to make sure he and his clients were taken care of. His thoughtfulness and appreciation for their work inspired the best from them.

Become involved professionally with your receptionist, and involve yourself in how she handles your appointment schedule. Above all, treat the receptionist with respect and she will take care of you.

"Accounting" For Success

Owning or operating a business requires responsibility—particularly financial responsibility. Frankly, fiscal accountability is the single most important skill you need to possess if you are to succeed as a self-employed business entrepreneur. It is a cold economic fact that 80 percent of all businesses fail during their first two years of operation.

Do not think for one moment that this section does not apply to you because you do not currently own a salon or because you rent the chair your clients sit in. Most hairdressers are or will become self-employed, owning and operating their own businesses. Therefore, you should take special note of this chapter— it does pertain to you.

Before you decide to change career fields, realize that I am not suggesting you need to become a certified public accountant or take courses in bookkeeping. Further, this section is not a lesson in business accounting.

If you want to learn the basics of accounting, there are plenty of books on the market that will train you; if you want to set up a business accounting program, there are several computer software tools that offer everything from basic accounting to payroll. What I will attempt to do is show you the value of finding and hiring an accounting professional for business success.

I have been a successful hairdresser for twenty-five years. During this time, I have always engaged the professional services of an accountant to help me run my business. Some of the services included are annual consultations and tax return preparations; advice on how to prepare quarterly, federal, and state tax statements; advice on how to complete monthly profit and loss statements; advice on how to structure overhead expenditures; budget development; and advice on how to meet other bookkeeping obligations.

Before you tune out of this chapter, let me say just this one thing: Every hair stylist who earns more than one hundred thousand a year in income runs his or her business like a business! This is part of that business. If you don't handle your accounting well, there is a good chance you will never see one hundred thousand a year in income. Get it? Keep reading.

Regardless of the extent of services received, retaining an accounting professional has helped me to keep more of the income I produced and has left me with plenty of free time to enjoy my family. These accounting services are necessary and take time to complete. I cannot place a value on the family time; I can, however, say with certainty that the income saved by my accountant far outweighs the cost for his services—that allows me to justify the yearly expense for an accountant. I know you'll agree, too.

Do not dismiss the importance of searching for the right accountant. Ask other hairdressers who they work with, or ask business professionals you trust for their recommendations. Put together a list of accountants and set up a consultation meeting with each of them. Take notes, and ask questions related to your situation. Essentially, you are interviewing them for the job. You are hiring them.

Avoid accountants who are too casual about IRS audits. Establish from the start that you want your financial records handled within the requirements of the law. Many accountants will go outside of what's legal and use loopholes to attract your business. Remember that every accountant will have you sign a document that states that they are not responsible for the information on your taxes and that they are only filing based on the information you gave them. Your accountant's rear end is covered! Once you sign your name to a "false" tax return, it is your future that is on the line, not the accountant's.

I have gone through several accountants over the years before I found the one I have now. He is confident, competent, and specializes in self-employed clients. Remember, however, that an accountant's value is dependent upon the records you provide him.

Meet your accountant with your records in your hand to get more services for your money. If an hourly fee is charged, organize your own records rather than paying the accountant to do it for you. If you pay a flat fee for his or her accounting services, time spent on the clerical chore of organizing records eats into the time that should be spent assessing your financial situation. Organize and maintain your business and personal records yourself.

What records should you maintain? Keep a list of all earnings. Include salary/commission, tips, dividends, interest, and net income. (Net income is the money you have left after all expenses.) Provide the accountant with the amounts and dates of any estimated tax payments (federal and state) that you have made. Keep copies of tax returns for the last seven years, and provide them to an accountant if you are using him or her for the first time. Compile a list of items you know are tax deductible, including medical expenses, mortgage interest payments, taxes, contributions, hairstyling tools, moving expenses, and business expenses in general.

Keep all of these records on your computer throughout the year. Update them at least every month so you don't have a large job to do at the end of the year. Remember that self-employed people generally have to file estimated tax payments each quarter. Talk to your accountant about how to set those up. This is very important and will prevent you from having a large tax bill all at once at the end of the year. If you are on payroll at a salon, ask your employer to adjust your withholdings to avoid end-of-year tax payments.

Financial success is your goal. To achieve it, you must make the correct choices. Don't make these choices alone. Get the help of an accountant who can streamline the financial side of your business and leave you time for the fun creative stuff.

Do I Open My Own Salon?

This short chapter will not teach you how to open your own salon. That would take up an entire book. But if salon ownership is an eventual goal of yours, put down your shears. You will not need them. Put on a new hat—a business hat. Many talented hair stylists open salons each year and do very well. Many, many more do not.

Here is the typical situation: You and a fellow stylist have been doing hair for years now, and both of you have a large clientele. You both know how to teach others to do hair, and you decide to get together and open a salon of your own. You both are making plenty of money; you're rock stars in your community. Why would you not open a salon?

It sounds pretty easy. You know about salons, you've worked in enough of them, and you know how to make a better salon than the one you are in. You have all of the product representatives' numbers, and they already told you they would help you set everything up. You're talented, and you know how to deal with hairdressers and clients.

The failure rate of small businesses in the first year is more than 80 percent. Of the rare 20 percent who make it through the first year, over 65 percent fail before five years have passed. Consider this fact: With the exception of restaurants, hair salons have the highest failure rate of all new businesses in the country. This is not because hairdressers have forgotten how to do hair or how to take care of clients. No, it's because they don't know how to run a business.

Running a hair salon has nothing to do with being able to do hair. Many basic business principles are involved, and many of those principles are used universally—you might as well have opened a shoe store. Operating a successful salon requires education; just as doing hair and building a clientele require education and experience, business ownership requires equal dedication and planning.

It may be your dream to someday work for yourself in your own salon. By all means, pursue your dream, but just as you did in the beginning, know what you're getting into and be prepared.

If you are serious about this, act seriously. Take courses at a local college that will help you, and read books on basic business principles. Talk to people who are running *profitable* salons and find out what has and hasn't worked for them. You should understand the principles of marketing, accounting, business organization, psychology, debt ratio, lease negotiations, and contracts, just to name a few. You don't have to be a master in these subjects to run a successful salon, but you can't be naïve and think that your dream alone will sail you to success. You have to study and be ready.

I've listed a few questions about business on the next page. The questions will get you thinking and hopefully give you some direction as to where you should start your education and how to prepare.

1. Based on the square footage of your salon, the number of income-producing stations, retail, and so forth, what is the income potential of the salon at 50 percent, 75 percent, and 100 percent capacity? (Capacity meaning the percentage of your stations that are filled.)

2. Based on your business plan, how long will it take you to reach each one of your income potential points? (50 percent, 75 percent, and 100 percent?)

3. How much is your initial investment going to be? This will include, but will not be limited to, interior build-out (interior construction—walls, floor, electrical, plumbing, heating/air, lighting, etc.), architectural drawings, city/county permits, all equipment (stations, chairs, etc.), and stocking initial retail and chemical products.

4. Based on your business plan, how long will it take you to break even? Do you have extra money to "float" the business until you can break even? What happens if it takes longer to break even than you projected it would?

5. Who is your accountant? (Not "do you have one?") Are you going to operate as a sole proprietorship, a corporation, or a limited liability company? Your accountant will explain the advantages and disadvantages of these choices.

6. Who is doing your payroll and your federal, state, and local tax deposits, withholdings, filings, and reports? (Get a

service! It's the best money you will ever spend.)

7. How much does your salon need to generate a day just to reach the break-even point?

8. How will you track your business progress and know if you're heading in the right direction? Will you simply gauge business health by the amount of clients in the chairs, or will you have a way to *know*?

9. Do you know your insurance expenses?

10. Have you factored your yearly property tax on all of your equipment into your business plan?

These few questions are not submitted to dismay or discourage you. They are intended to be thought provoking and to give you a small look at the skill set required to run a business— even a hair salon.

I opened my first salon at the age of twenty-two. I had been in the hair business for less than two years at that point. Throughout my career, I always saw myself as a businessperson who happened to be good at doing hair, not a as hairdresser who owned a business.

There is a huge distinction between the two points of view.

My advice to anyone starting in this industry is to set yourself apart from the crowd. Get the extra education and acquire the skill sets that you'll need to build and maintain a large and profitable clientele. Do what is necessary to give yourself the edge so you don't end up in the large percentage of hair stylists who never succeed in the business. My advice is the same for anybody interested in opening a salon of his or her own. Know that running a salon is an entirely separate job. It has nothing to do with being able to do hair. So just as you did in the beginning, get the education and train yourself to be successful in this job, and make sure that you don't fall into that pit of the huge percentage of people who fail. If you do what is necessary and prepare yourself, you will not fall into that statistic. You will have a successful business, and you will help the industry as a whole.

Exit Plan

So now you're in it. You're living the dream. You've managed to beat the odds, and you're actually making a very comfortable living doing something you love. You've built and maintained the clientele, and you've passed down your knowledge to others. Perhaps you have even opened your own salon and are truly now the master of your own destiny.

What now? Where do you go from here? You own your home, you drive a nice car, and you can vacation and have the lifestyle that you always wanted. What now? What is the plan? Is there one? I will ask the simple and scary question: How long will you do hair, and what will you do after?

I'll tell you a true story. My wife, Krisztina, was born in Hungary. She has a wonderful uncle named Geza. As I write this, he is ninety-five years old. He escaped and immigrated to the United States from communist Hungary in 1956. He didn't have a penny to his name when he came here, but he had a trade. He is a hair stylist. While he was in the refugee camp waiting for his visa to be approved, he offered five-cent haircuts to anyone he could talk to. He worked very hard and saved everything. Over the course of months in the camp, he managed to save thirty-five dollars. He used that money to begin his life here in America. Geza recently retired from the business in Dallas, Texas, and before he retired at the age of ninety-five, he was still doing hair three days a week. (If you search online, you may still be able to find the local news story about him and his retirement from his position as the oldest hair stylist in Texas.)

One day, Geza and I were talking about business, comparing notes, and talking "hair" in general. He asked me if my clientele was still strong. I told him that I was very blessed and that it was. He told me he had lost a lot of clients lately. I tried to reassure him that clients come and go, a fact that he knows well. I told him to stay consistent and to not let it bother him. "No, you don't understand," he said. "I'm losing them to the graveyard." Up until recently, he would schedule his guests in fifteen-minute increments. He would set the rollers for one while one was under the dryer. Then he would quickly comb out the next.

That has been his way of doing things for as long as he can remember. It's been a good career. He's always made a good living, and most importantly, he's enjoyed it along the way. The thought of doing something else never crossed his mind. He has been truly blessed in that respect.

So here's the question again: How long will you do hair, and what will you do after? Most people, myself included, don't have the tenacity to work in the hair industry for that length of time—at least not "behind the chair." Don't get me wrong: there are far worse ways to make a living. The hair industry is wonderful and has provided my family and me with a terrific living and lifestyle for twenty-five years. Considering the fact that I was just a dumb kid from Los Angeles who never went to college, I can't complain a bit.

Years ago I met a brilliant man named Michael Cole. His contributions to the hair industry are unbelievable. I was attending a weeklong training seminar of his in Minneapolis. After the class was finished for the day, he sat and talked to me awhile. During the course of our conversation, he asked me a very direct question that I had never thought of before. He said, "Alan, what is your exit strategy?" I didn't understand the question at first. There I was, taking a course to learn about building my salons further and how to be a more successful salon owner. I wasn't expecting a question regarding my exit plans from the industry. Michael has had a stellar career in every facet of the beauty industry for decades. He explained that he wasn't referring to my leaving the hair industry. He was talking about actually working "behind the chair."

The point of the story is not the answer to his question or the conclusion I came to. The point is that it made me consider something that had never occurred to me in the past. Why would I have thought of that anyway? Again, I'm in it. I'm living the dream and enjoying a great lifestyle because of this industry. Well, the question needed to be asked, and I'm grateful he asked it.

I put these ideas to words merely to get you thinking. We can't all be Uncle Geza. This industry offers a level of freedom that few others can offer. How many people can say that they visit and laugh with people every day and get paid for it? How many can literally make their own schedule and work when they want to? This industry is amazing on many, many levels, but unless your career plans mirror Uncle Geza's, you need to have an exit plan.

The good news is this: you have lots and lots of time to think about it. Have fun meeting all of the new people you'll come into contact with. Enjoy the clientele you have worked hard to build and maintain. Learn from them. Enjoy the people you work with. Stay professional at all times, and keep your integrity and your cool. I believe you have an obligation to pass on what you have learned; enjoy that process too. It will be more rewarding than you could imagine.

God bless,

Alan Daniels

Made in the USA
San Bernardino, CA
13 March 2016